RUDIMENTAL DRUM SOLOS

FOR THE MARCHING SNARE DRUMMER

by Ben Hans

ISBN 978-0-634-06056-4

7777 W. BLUEMOUND RD. P.O. BOX 13819 MILWAUKEE, WI 53213

In Australia Contact:
Hal Leonard Australia Pty. Ltd.
4 Lentara Court
Cheltenham, Victoria, 3192 Australia
Email: ausadmin@halleonard.com.au

Visit Hal Leonard Online at
www.halleonard.com

ABOUT THE AUTHOR

Ben Hans is a musician and music instructor in the greater Milwaukee, Wisconsin area. In addition to keeping a busy performance schedule throughout the upper Midwest, Ben teaches music classes and percussion studies at the Milwaukee Area Technical College, and also instructs more than 50 private music students. With teaching experience at the elementary, intermediate, high school, and collegiate levels, Ben continues to be an assistant to many intermediate and high school band directors and programs.

An active member of the Percussive Arts Society, Ben holds an Associate's Degree in Music from the Milwaukee Area Technical College, and a Bachelor's Degree in Music from the University of Wisconsin. Ben is an adjudicator and charter member of the I.A.T.D. (International Association of Traditional Drummers), examined by drumming legend John S. Pratt. In addition to leading his own jazz trio, Ben performs regularly as a freelance artist. He endorses Istanbul Agop cymbals and is the author of two other titles published by Hal Leonard Corporation: *Workin' Drums: 50 Solos for Drumset* and *40 Intermediate Snare Drum Solos*.

Any questions or comments regarding the contents of this book can be directed to the author via the internet at www.benhans.com.

DEDICATION

To my students past and present, may you continue to strive for excellence in life and in the study of percussion.

To John S. "Jack" Pratt, a man whose knowledge, wisdom, creative genius, and skill are eclipsed only by his kindness and generosity. Thanks, Jack!

FOREWORD

For as long as I have known him, Ben Hans has shown me his special interest in the performance of our 26 Standard American Drumming Rudiments as a key to building a strong and fluid technical style. He has also devoted himself to studying the historical development of the art of Traditional Drumming, not only in the United States, but in foreign countries as well. Ben's devotion to drumming has been one of dedication and development, and his newest book, ***Rudimental Solos for the Marching Snare Drummer***, is an absolutely splendid example that his quality of percussive perfection will provide necessary challenges for a drummer's improvement.

John S. Pratt
Hawthorne, NJ

CONTENTS

About This Book 4
- To The Player 4
- To The Instructor 5
- Notation Legend 5
- About Rudimental Drumming 6

Introduction 7
- Percussive Arts Society International Drum Rudiments 8

Focus on Five I 10
1. Single Stroke Roll 10
2. Double Stroke Open Roll (Long Roll) 10
3. Single Paradiddle 10
4. Double Paradiddle 10
5. Flam 10

First Stage 11
Ground Work 12
Flam Mission 13
Focus on Five II 14
1. Drag (Ruff) 14
2. Single Drag Tap (Single Drag) 14
3. Five Stroke Roll 14
4. Seven Stroke Roll 14
5. Nine Stroke Roll 14

Double-Up 16
San Diego Street Beat 18
Reach Out and Gimme Five 20
Focus on Five III 21
1. Flam Tap 21
2. Ten Stroke Roll 21
3. Flamacue 21
4. Thirteen Stroke Roll 21
5. Fifteen Stroke Roll 21

Memorial Day Parade 22
Jackson Square 23
Old Cape Henry 24
Focus on Five IV 26
1. Flam Accent 26
2. Single Ratamacue 26
3. Double Drag Tap (Double Drag) 26
4. Double Ratamacue 26
5. Lesson 25 26

Speightstown Stomp 28
Bridge over Chesapeake 30
Dustin' off the Chops 32
Focus on Five V 34
1. Drag Paradiddle #1 34
2. Flam Paradiddle 34
3. Drag Paradidle #2 34
4. Flam Paradiddle-Diddle 34
5. Triple Ratamacue 34

Standing on the Shoulders of Giants 35
Myla's March 38
Focus on Five VI 40
1. Six Stroke Roll 40
2. Eleven Stroke Roll 40
3. Seventeen Stroke Roll 40
4. Triple Paradiddle 40
5. Single Paradiddle-Diddle 40

Ease into It 42
The Wanderer 44
Double Dribble Diddle 46
Focus on Five VII 48
1. Multiple Bounce Roll 48
2. Single Stroke of Seven 48
3. Triple Stroke Roll 48
4. Single Stroke of Four 48
5. Dragadiddle 48

Atop Fort Rodney 49
Sammie's Samba 50
Beehive 52
Focus on Five VIII 54
1. Swiss Army Triplet 54
2. Inverted Flam Tap 54
3. Pataflafla 54
4. Single Flammed Mill 54
5. Flam Drag 54

Tambor Con Cuarenta En Bolero 56
Sir Lowery's Pass 58
The Beach 60
Focus on Five IX: Hybrid Rudiments 62
1. Double Dragadiddle 62
2. Ruff Double Paradiddle 62
3. Two Stroke Ruff Paradiddle-Diddle 62
4. Flam Double Paradiddle 62
5. Three Stroke Ruff Paradiddle-Diddle 62

Queen Anne's Revenge 64
Focus on Five X: Swiss and Hybrid Rudiments 66
1. Cheese (or Flam Stutters) 66
2. Cheese Paradiddle 66
3. Flammed Five Stroke Roll (or Flam Fives) 66
4. Four Stroke Ruff Single Ratamacue 66
5. Flammed Nine Stroke Roll 66

Bucky Wagon 68
Focus on Five XI: Hybrid Rudiments 70
1. Four Stroke Ruff Single Paradiddle 70
2. Inverted Paraddle-Diddle 70
3. Berger Lesson 25 70
4. Double Windmill Stroke 70
5. Four Stroke Ruff Double Ratamacue 70

E-Gad, Inverted Paradiddle-Diddles!? 72
Select Bibliography 74
Glossary 76

ABOUT THIS BOOK

To the Player

Congratulations on continuing your quest to become a better drummer. *Rudimental Solos for the Marching Snare Drummer* is a starting point on your quest toward excellence. For the purpose of expanding one's repertoire, additional rudiments beyond the 40 Percussive Arts Society list have been included in this book. I have attempted to compose pieces that will sound musical within the snare drum idiom, while still accessible as teaching aids. I hope that you will find use for the music, exercises, and information contained herein. Remember, this book is only a stepping stone in your quest to become a master drummer. Investigate and perform this art form as much as possible.

This book is not an end in itself, but is an aid to use in your journey to achive drumming prowess. Start at the beginning of the book and work progressively, unit by unit, and practice every day. Also read and play from rudimental methods and other solo material (see the bibliography). It is only with constant, steady, and correct practice that you will improve. There are no shortcuts! Be patient and persistent in your quest, and don't be afraid to enlist the assistance of a qualified teacher. Remember: have fun! The future of this great art form is now in your hands.

To the up-and-coming rudimental drummer, it is very important to have a correct interpretation of not only what is current and valid in today's music and drumming, but to have a correct interpretation of its foundations. It is just as important to develop an understanding of styles and periods on the snare drum as it is to understand the styles and periods on the drum set, marimba, xylophone, and vibraphone. A historic and factual approach to period music on your instrument is just as important as musicians who study instruments like the trumpet, saxophone, or piano, etc. Every instrument has a line of invention, development, descendancy, and various musical adoptions.

For the purpose of study I have written 26 etudes that contain the rudiments of drumming, the roots of which can be traced back over seven centuries. As a student of percussion and a rudimental drummer, it is up to you to correctly interpret, understand, perform, and pass on our art of rudimental drumming.

With regard to the content of this book, don't ignore some rudiments because they do not appear in your marching band music. As a soloist and rudimentalist, you must understand that not all rudiments are used in today's modern marching band arrangements. Learn all the rudiments and don't be fooled into the classic and often-repeated line, "*That's too old-school for me. I don't need to work on ratamacues*." Yes, there is some truth to the thought that traditional rudimental drumming sounds a certain way, but you need to learn it. It is the foundation. One cannot advance if one does not know or understand what has happened in the past. Mastering literature by Schinstine, Wilcoxin, and Pratt is as important as mastering newer literature by Hurley, Frytag, and Queen. Learn from all periods and don't ignore the classics. Be the best drummer you can be by making sure you understand the heritage of our instrument. I encourage you, as a student of the drums, to learn as much as possible about the history, traditions, and current trends in rudimental drumming. You can get started with some of the selections in the bibliography of this text. Perform a web search for "hybrid rudiments," go to performances, watch drumming videos, and obtain rudimental recordings. Expose yourself to this art as much as possible. Don't settle for mediocrity in your playing. Practice daily and often, and work toward a goal of mastering first the 26 N.A.R.D. rudiments (the foundation), and then the 40 P.A.S. rudiments (the next foundation). Only upon mastering these concepts should you move on to more complex Swiss and hybrid rudiments.

It is also very important to practice individual rudiments in rudimental breakdowns, from slow to fast to slow: open, close, open.

As a drummer, you need to know not only how to play fast and loud, but how to play with dynamics, form, and musicality. You need to play just as musically as one would on any other instrument.

To the Instructor

After many conversations with my peers in the elementary, secondary, and collegiate level music teaching professions, I have deduced that a progressive rudimental teaching aid is in great demand; not simply another collection of solo works, but something that can aid in the progression of learning rudiments in a fun, challenging, and musical manner. What is needed is something that can get the hands moving in the right direction. One of the most challenging tasks for many band directors is how to introduce, explain, and work the rudiments. I have designed each unit in this book as a module of cumulative progression. There are first, five rudiments to master ("Focus on Five"), then exercises and etudes, then ten rudiments to master, followed by exercises and etudes, followed by 15, and so on. This book contains the rudiments in a more traditional form. It is important to learn the correct phrasing of grace notes, so I have chosen to notate the music utilizing traditional notation. A word of caution: in this collection of snare drum music, I have included additional drum rudiments beyond the 40 P.A.S. rudiments. I have attempted to compose pieces that will sound musical within the snare drum idiom, while teaching rudiments at the same time. It is my hope that the material herein will be a reliable and resourceful aid to you the teacher, you the advanced rudamentalist, or you the professional.

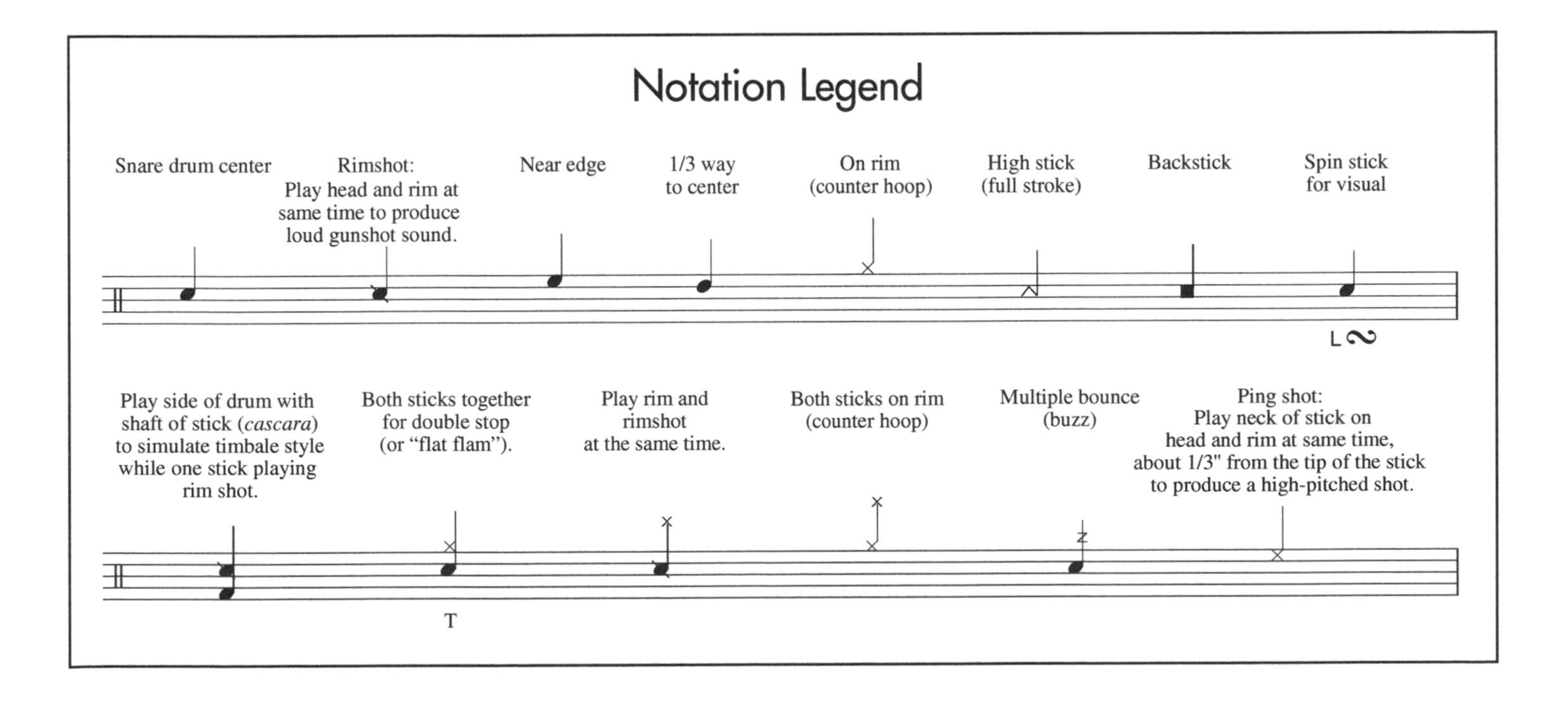

About Rudimental Drumming

Stylistic differences are all about interpretation. In certain cases, some music notation can be incredibly vague. Listen to rudimental drumming recordings and watch rudimental drumming videos to compare the differences that exist.

For instance, there are several ways to interpret the drag and four-stroke ruff:

For the purpose of this book, perform the drag "up next to the beat" when notated like this: (traditional), not "in time" or "on" the mathematical beat. When notated like this (contemporary), play on the beat. For more information, see section 31, page 109 of Dr. John Wooten's *The Drummer's Rudimental Reference Book* and *Drag Interpretation for the Rudimental Drummer* by Dan C. Spaulding.

Realize that at very fast tempos like those tempos performed in the modern contemporary drum lines, the grace note of a drag flattens out "in time," just as the swing of the jazz ride cymbal will flatten out at high tempos from to very fast .

Be aware of the four stroke ruff "up next to the beat" feeling of three grace notes vs. the "in time" or "on" the beat feeling of . See the *Percussive Arts Society International Drum Rudiments* book for more information.

Know that there are sometimes differences in the stickings of grace notes, depending on the country's interpretations of graces, RRR L or RLL R or RRL L. See *A Study of the Rudiments Used in Foreign Military Drumming Styles*, by John K. Galm and *Accents and Rebounds* by George Stone, page 21, for additional information.

There can also be a difference in the approach to a grace note in the three stroke ruff, RL R / LR L. See *Reading Exercises for Snare Drum*, page 9, by Bob Tilles or *Percussion Education Department* by James D. Salmon under "Three Stroke Ruff" and compare to hybrids, page 121, of *The Next Level: Rudimental Snare Drum Techniques* by Jeff Queen. Compare the feeling of "on the beat" compared to "up next to the beat."

INTRODUCTION

Throughout the history of human civilization, each generation has benefited from the knowledge, discoveries, and learnings of the generations that came before them. In music, this is also true. Composers, performers, and instrument inventors of the past have given us the foundations that are being used to this day. In rudimental drumming, this is also true. Drum composers, performers, and instrument inventors have provided a basis of drumming foundations that are very important to today's drummer.

The snare drum evolved from the earliest adaptation of Middle-Eastern drums to early European snare drums and to eventual use in the Swiss military. Swiss military drumming spread throughout Europe, and eventually found its way to the United States during the Revolutionary War era. The drum has changed greatly from the early construction of rope-tensioned instruments made of hide and wood, to the 20th century's inventions of metal counter hoops, metal tension rods, and Mylar heads, to today's free-floating snare drums with Kevlar heads. The snare drum has truly evolved, and so has the music.

In American drumming, because of varied teaching methods and techniques of playing that carried over from the 19th century, an effort was made in the 20th century to standardize rudimental training for the next generation of drummers. Such publications as Charles Ashworth's *System of Drum Beating* (1812) and Bruce and Emmett's *Drummers' and Fifers' Guide* (1862) included rudiments, but an American standard was set by the N.A.R.D. (National Association of Rudimental Drumming). This group of 13 drummers and professional percussionists included the great J. Burns Moore, George Lawrence Stone, and William F. Ludwig, among others. On June 20, 1933, at the American Legion Convention in Chicago, Illinois, this group decided on the 13 essential rudiments of American drumming, which was soon after doubled to 26. Most of these rudiments had already been in common use, but the N.A.R.D. list set the standards for American rudimental drummers for much of the 20th century.

The 26 N.A.R.D. rudiments were standard practice for many decades, until the 1980s, when after many years of discussion and debate within the percussion community, a notable group of rudimental drummers and professional percussionists from the P.A.S. (Percussive Arts Society) increased the number of rudiments on the list. This group included Jay Wanamaker, Anthony Cirone, and William F. Ludwig II, who formed a rudimental drum committee to update and add to the 26 N.A.R.D. drum rudiments (by that time the N.A.R.D. as an association was defunct). Fourteen rudiments were added to the N.A.R.D. list, which was now deemed the "40 P.A.S. International Snare Drum Rudiments." The P.A.S. committee added several of the Swiss drum rudiments, which had become standard practice in drum lines, as well as several "orchestral" rudiments. This occurred much to the satisfaction of many modern contemporary drummers, and much to the chagrin of many traditionalists.

Since we entered the 21st century, many changes and adaptations have occurred within the bounds of rudimental drumming, as well as movements to promote the heritage of our instrument. Recently, rudimental drummer and celebrated author John S. Pratt founded a group of traditional drummers called The International Association of Traditional Drummers (I.A.T.D.) that would work to reinforce the foundation of rudimental drumming. Many organized groups of rudamentalists exist across the country that promote the heritage of rudimental drumming. Some examples include the American Patriots Rudimental Drummers Club (A.P.R.D.C.) of Morgantown, Pennsylvania, and internationally, the Canadian Associates Drumming Rudimental Excellence (C.A.D.R.E.). Since the 1970s, Drum Corps International (D.C.I.) continues to set the highest standard of excellence in marching percussion, and, in addition to many fine American college marching lines, continues to develop many new and hybrid combinations each year. Many lines have their own nicknames for endless variations of rudiments.

Truth be told, there are literally hundreds upon hundreds of drum rudiments. Many countries have their own unique tradition of drumming, and each their own rudimental language. Many of the hybrids and other non-P.A.S. listed drum rudiments are simply combinations or permutations of the existing drum rudiments. Some are actually other countries' rudiments. There are thousands of lists made up of many exciting permutations. It may well be time to add another group of rudiments to our current P.A.S. list, a standardized list for the advanced rudimental drummer. This will be a difficult, but much-needed task to accomplish. Many of the so-called hybrids have different names in different drum lines and in different regions of the United States. Some rudiments are simply European in origin, given a different name in U.S. drum lines. An effort should be made to uphold the correct and traditional names of these rudiments.

A 1982 article from the P.A.S. Rudiment Committee proposing the 40 P.A.S. rudiments stated, "This listing will be revised and updated in the future when needed." Maybe another P.A.S. standardized list of drumming rudiments is needed, including rudiments this author has played from various solo literature, and has seen firsthand, performed at field shows and at the snare drum solo finals of the annual P.A.S. convention. In any case, one thing can be said: of all the great drumming going on today, we can be sure that we are enjoying our rudimental art form thanks to the hard work, dedication, and love of the instrument of all those great players, composers, and teachers that have come before.

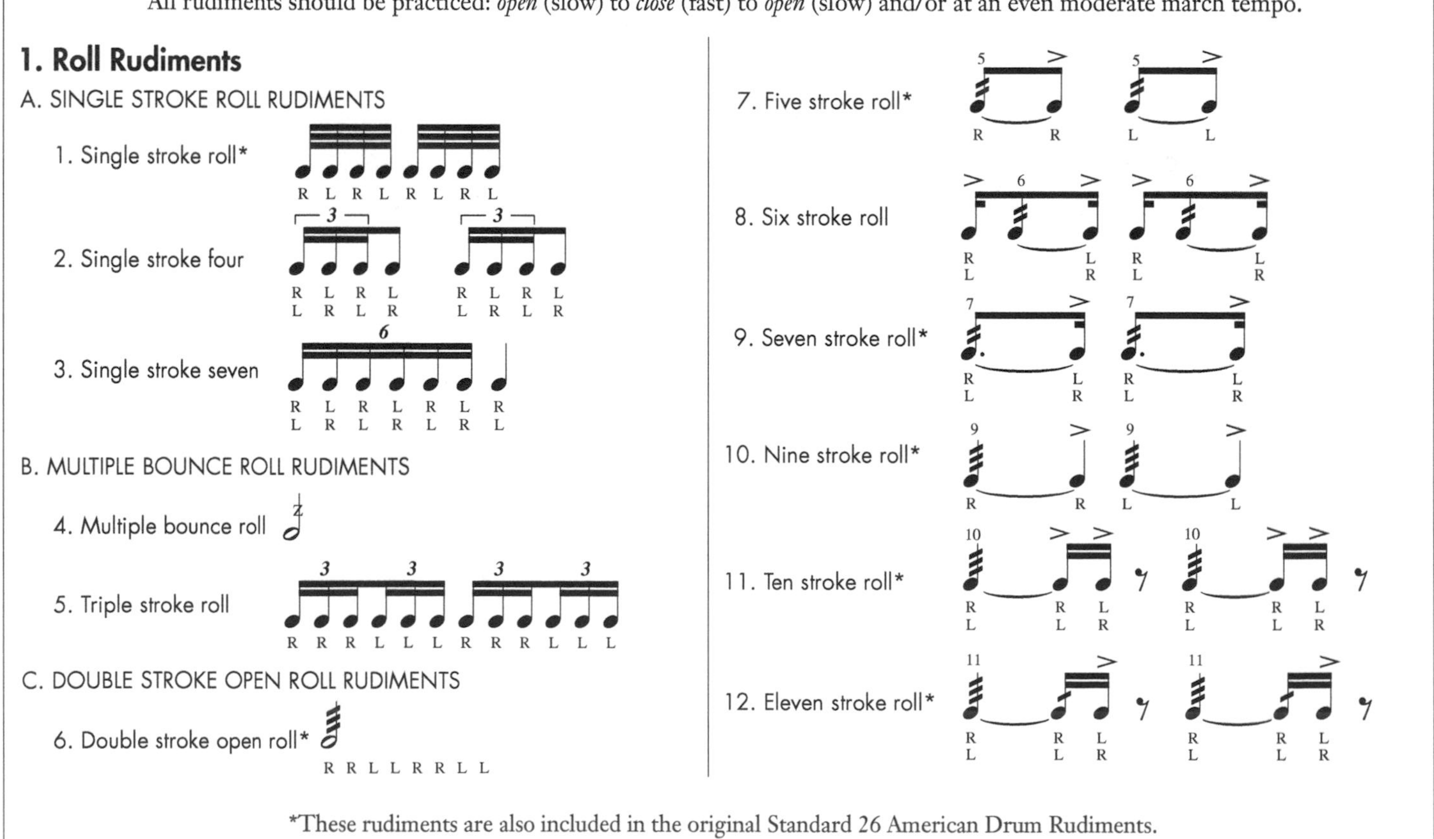

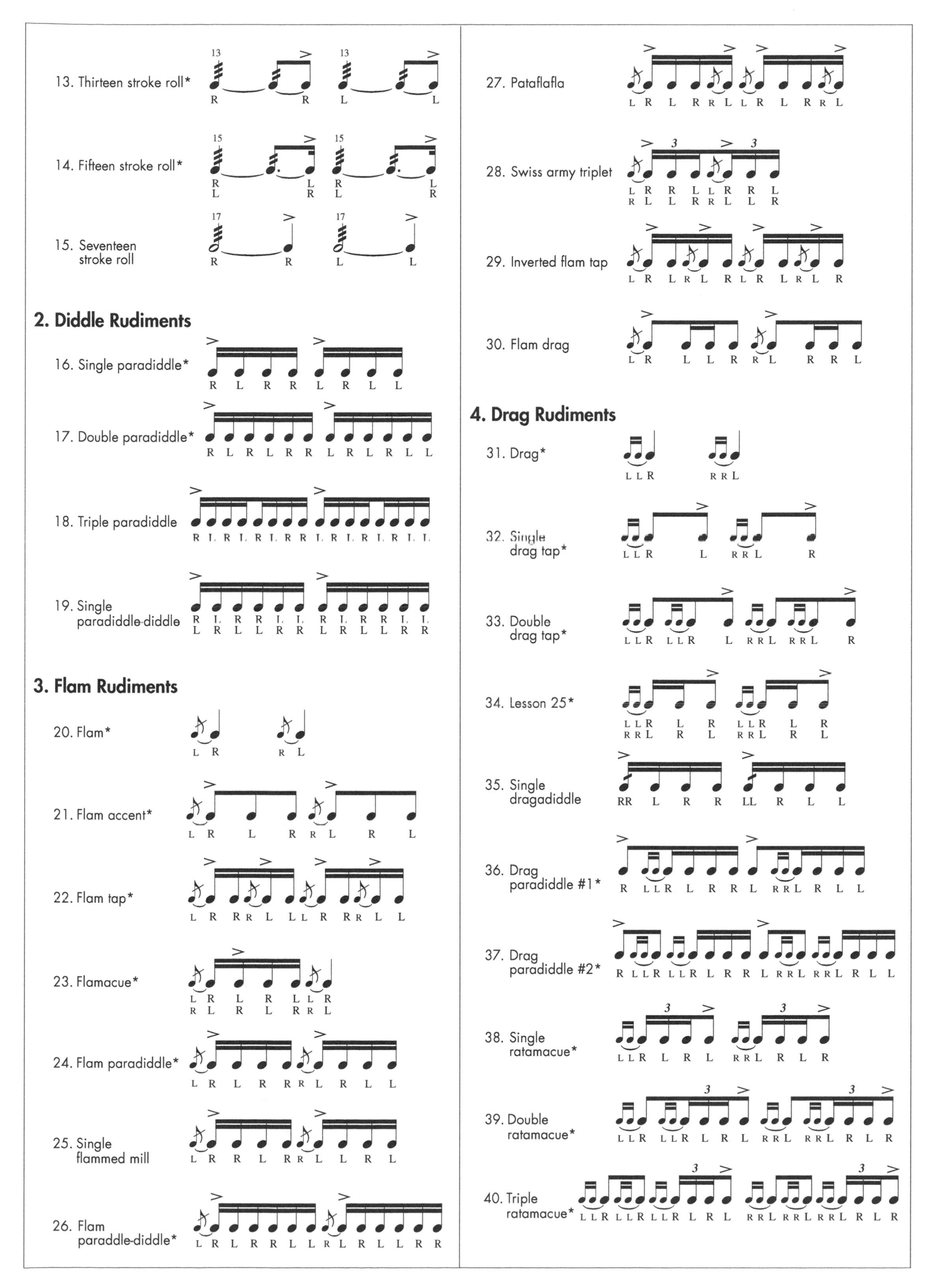
13. Thirteen stroke roll*
13 13
R R L L
14. Fifteen stroke roll*
15 15
R L L R R L L R
15. Seventeen stroke roll
17 17
R R L L
2. Diddle Rudiments
16. Single paradiddle*
R L R R L R L L
17. Double paradiddle*
R L R L R R L R L R L L
18. Triple paradiddle
R L R L R L R R L R L R L R L L
19. Single paradiddle-diddle
R L R R L L R L R R L L
L R L L R R L R L L R R
3. Flam Rudiments
20. Flam*
L R R L
21. Flam accent*
L R L R R L R L
22. Flam tap*
L R R R L L L R R R L L
23. Flamacue*
L R L R L L R
R L R L R R L
24. Flam paradiddle*
L R L R R R L R L L
25. Single flammed mill
L R R L R R L L R L
26. Flam paraddle-diddle*
L R L R R L L R L R L L R R
27. Pataflafla
L R L R R L L R L R R L
28. Swiss army triplet
3 3
L R R L L R R L
R L L R R L L R
29. Inverted flam tap
L R L R L R L R L R L R
30. Flam drag
L R L L R R L R R L
4. Drag Rudiments
31. Drag*
L L R R R L
32. Single drag tap*
L L R L R R L R
33. Double drag tap*
L L R L L R L R R L R R L R
34. Lesson 25*
L L R L R L L R L R
R R L R L R R L R L
35. Single dragadiddle
RR L R R LL R L L
36. Drag paradiddle #1*
R L L R L R R L R R L R L L
37. Drag paradiddle #2*
R L L R L L R L R R L R R L R R L R L L
38. Single ratamacue*
3 3
L L R L R L R R L R L R
39. Double ratamacue*
3 3
L L R L L R L R L R R L R R L R L R
40. Triple ratamacue*
3 3
L L R L L R L L R L R L R R L R R L R R L R L R

FOCUS ON FIVE I

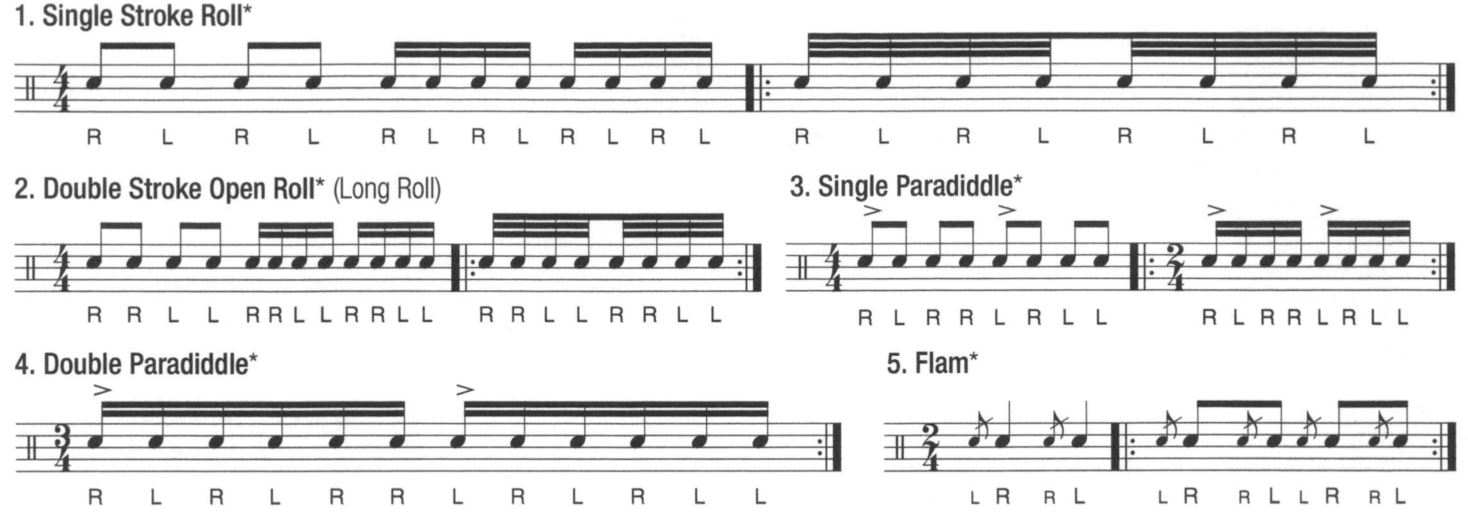

*Denotes rudiments included in the original (N.A.R.D.) Standard 26 American Drum Rudiments.

PRACTICE TIPS

- Practice each rudiment open (slow) to close (fast) to open (slow).
- Get a relaxed, even feel.
- Repeat each exercise 20 times or more.
- Add accents for increased dexterity.
- Tag each exercise below with a quarter note in the opposite hand.
- Create your own sticking for more fun variations.

Rudiment Warm-Ups

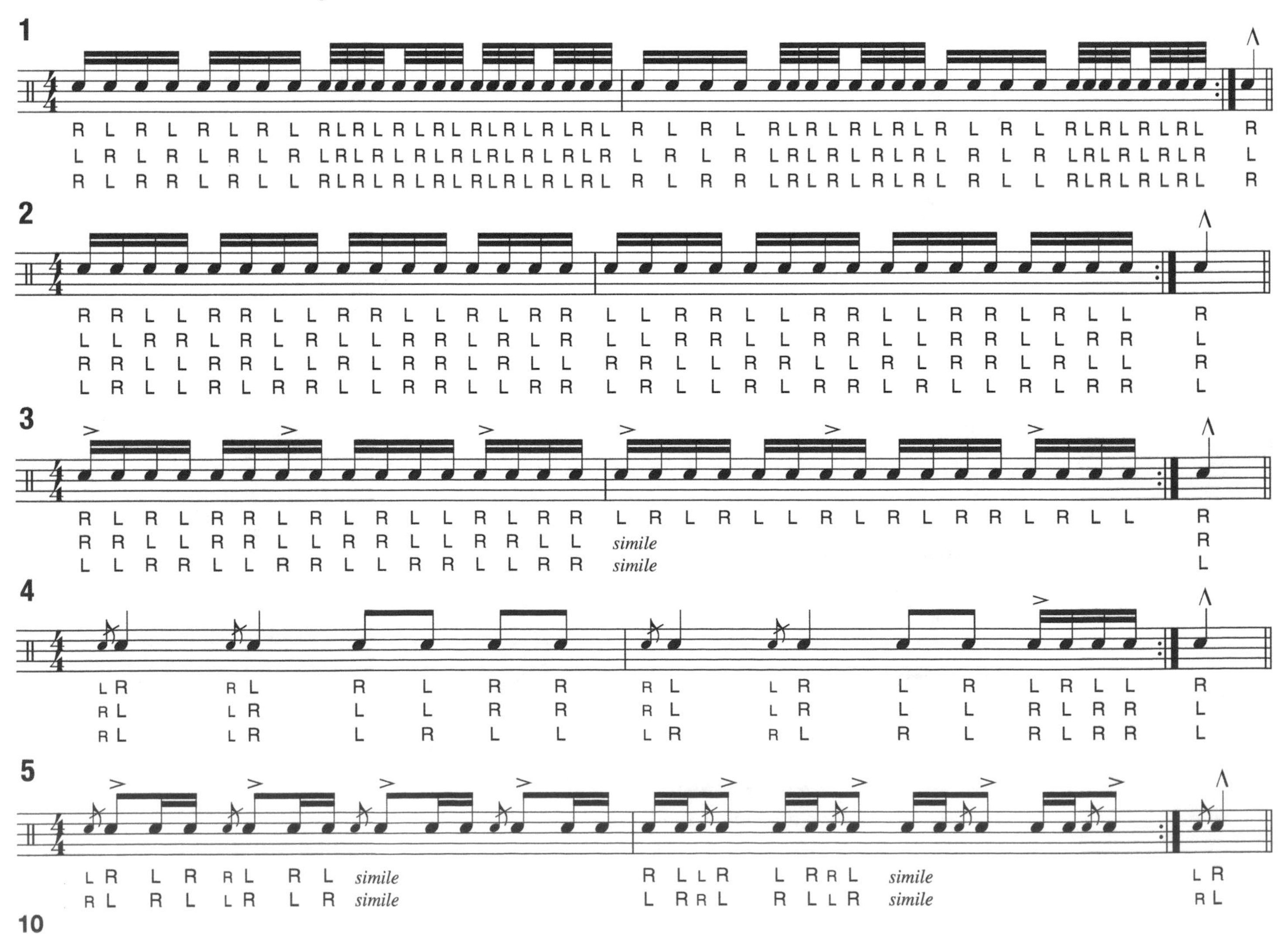

PERFORMANCE TIPS

- Try to attain the left hand lead at measures 23–24. (Alternate sticking may be used as a substitute.)
- Be sure to count syncopated rhythms at letter D.

GROUND WORK

PERFORMANCE TIPS

- Pay close attention to single strokes and accents.
- Switch your lead to left hand at letter C on repeat.
- Be careful at letter E; make sure to count.

FLAM MISSION

PERFORMANCE TIPS

- Switch hand lead on first repeat of A.
- Work up letter B slowly at first.
- Play right hand lead on D.C.

By BEN HANS

FOCUS ON FIVE II

[1] See page 6 for comments.

* Denotes rudiments included in the original (N.A.R.D.) Standard 26 American Drum Rudiments.

Notes:

PRACTICE TIPS

- Play slowly at first.
- Use accents.
- Attain an even roll with both hands.
- Repeat exercise below 20 times or more, then change lead.

Rudiment Warm-Ups

DOUBLE-UP

PERFORMANCE TIPS

- Play left hand lead at letter C repeat.
- Make sure to play cleanly at measures 37–38.

By BEN HANS

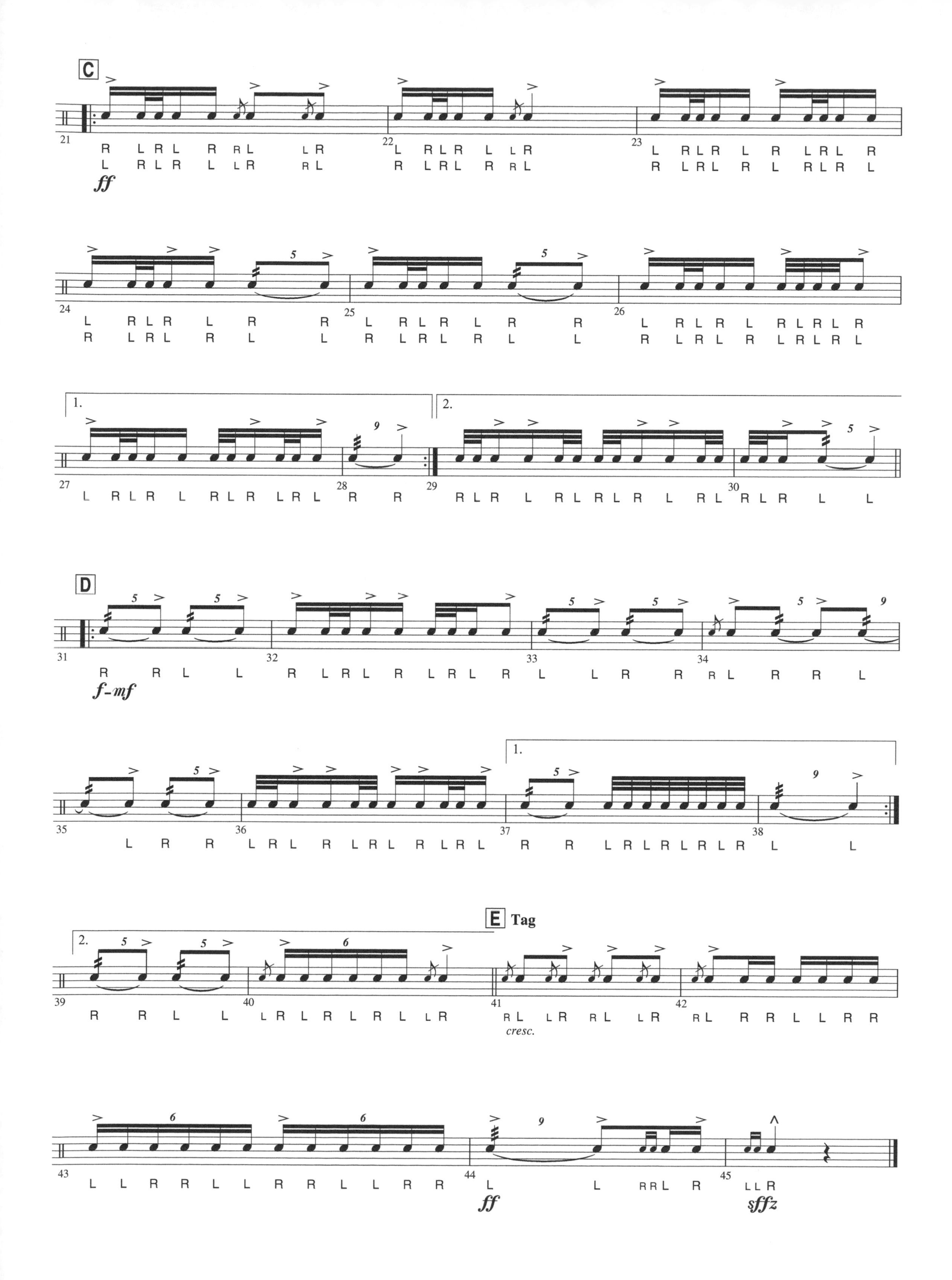
C
21
R L R L R R L L R
L R L R L L R R L
ff
22
L R L R L L R
R L R L R R L
23
L R L R L R L R L R
R L R L R L R L R L
24
L R L R L R R
R L R L R L L
25
L R L R L R R
R L R L R L L
26
L R L R L R L R L R
R L R L R L R L R L
1.
27
L R L R L R L R L R L
28
R R
2.
29
R L R L R L R L R L R L
30
R L R L L
D
31
R R L L
f-mf
32
R L R L R L R L R
33
L L R R
34
R L R R L
35
L R R
36
L R L R L R L R L R L
1.
37
R R L R L R L R L R
38
L L
E Tag
2.
39
R R L L
40
L R L R L R L L R
41
R L L R R L L R
cresc.
42
R L R R L L R R
43
L L R R L L R R L L R R
44
L
ff
L R R L R
45
L L R
sffz

SAN DIEGO STREET BEAT

PERFORMANCE TIPS

- Be sure rhythm is counted and played cleanly in measure 24.
- Don't slow down at measure 27.
- Practice this solo slowly to achieve correct phrasing in rolls, drags and diddles.

By BEN HANS

D
To Coda
D.S. al Coda
Coda
Presto!
ritard.
cresc.
ff
mp
mf
f
fff
sfz
sffz

REACH OUT AND GIMME FIVE

By BEN HANS

FOCUS ON FIVE III

PRACTICE TIPS

- Play all accents.
- Remember to play slowly first.
- Speed up only when learned slowly.
- Play rolls evenly with both hands.
- Look at Dominick Cuccia's book *The Beat of a Different Drummer* for more roll applications.

Rudiment Warm-Ups

MEMORIAL DAY PARADE

(Dedicated to the United States Veterans of Foreign Wars)

PERFORMANCE TIPS

- Although this solo is easier, maintain a strong pulse, and use accents to embellish the groove.
- Make sure measures 26–28 are even, as they are led with the left hand.

By BEN HANS

JACKSON SQUARE

PERFORMANCE TIPS

- Be cautious counting quintuplets.
- Play slowly at measure 33 with right hand high while spinning left stick, then accelerate.

OLD CAPE HENRY

PERFORMANCE TIPS

- Play all dynamics.
- Be sure to count when entering into letter C and the ten stroke rolls.

By BEN HANS

C
R L R L L R L R L R L L R L
mf-f cresc.
R R L R L L R L R L L R L R L L R L
R R L R L L R L R R L R L L R L
R R L R L L R L R L L R L R L L R LLRR
ff
LL RR L R R L RR LL RR LL R L L R LL RR
LL RR L R R L R LL RR LL RR L R R L RR LL
RR LL R L L R L L RR LL RR LL R L
L R LL RR LL RR L R R L RR LL RR LL R L
D
L R L R L L R L R R L R L L R L
f
R R L R L L R R R L L L R L
R LL RR LL RR L R R L RR LL RR LL R L
ff
L R R R L L L R R R L L L R L
R L
D.S. al Coda
R L
fp
R R L R L L R R R L L R L R L L R R R L
L R L R L L R R R L L R R L L R L
Coda
L R L L R
mp cresc.
R L R L L R L R L R R L L L L R R L
L R L R L
fp
fp
R R L R L L R L R L R L R L R L R
ff
sffz

FOCUS ON FIVE IV

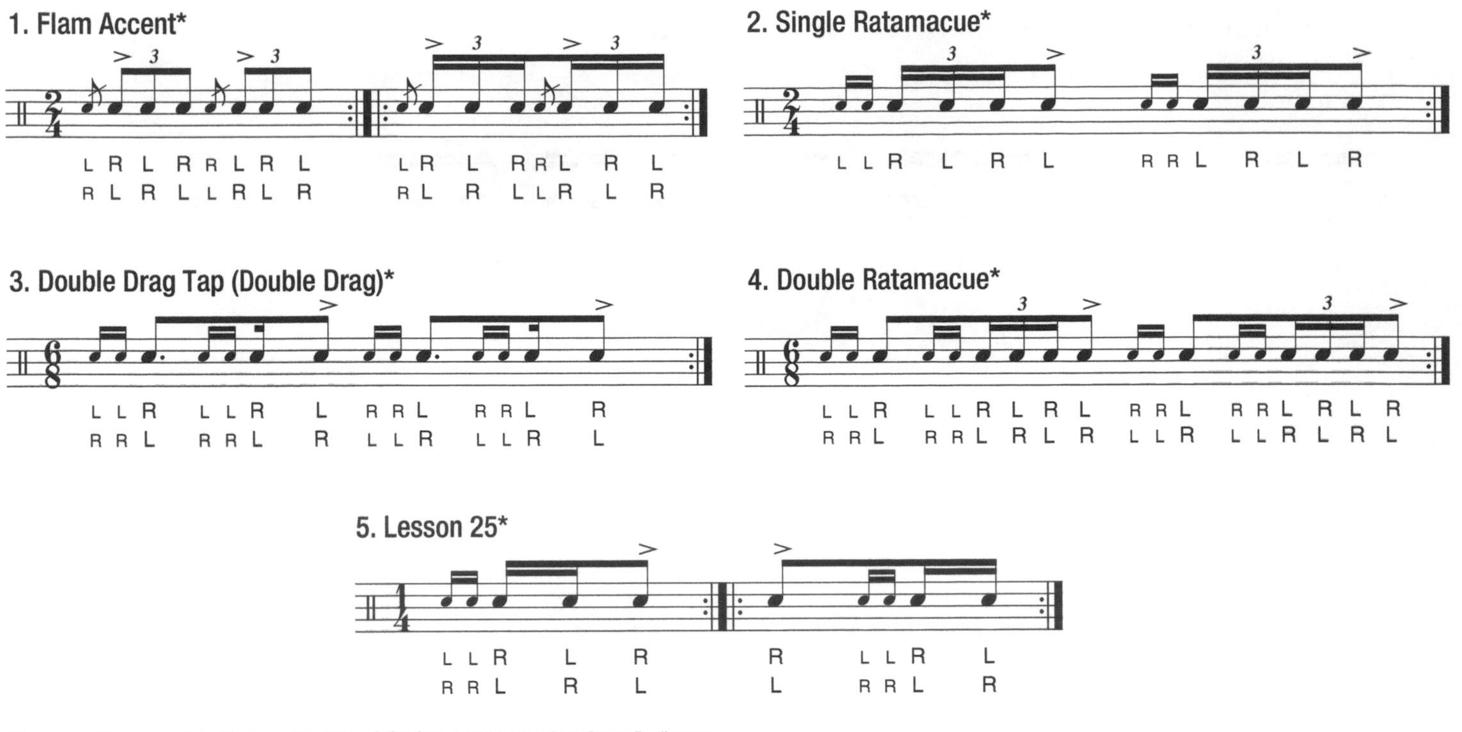

*Denotes rudiments included in the original (N.A.R.D.) Standard 26 American Drum Rudiments.

Notes:

PRACTICE TIPS

- Play all accents.
- Add your own dynamics.
- Play slow to fast.
- Write your own combinations.
- Repeat each exercise 20 times or more.

Rudiment Warm-Ups

SPEIGHTSTOWN STOMP

PERFORMANCE TIPS

- Practice letter D without graces and think of a syncopated Caribbean beat.
- After learning the rhythm, add the grace notes.

By BEN HANS

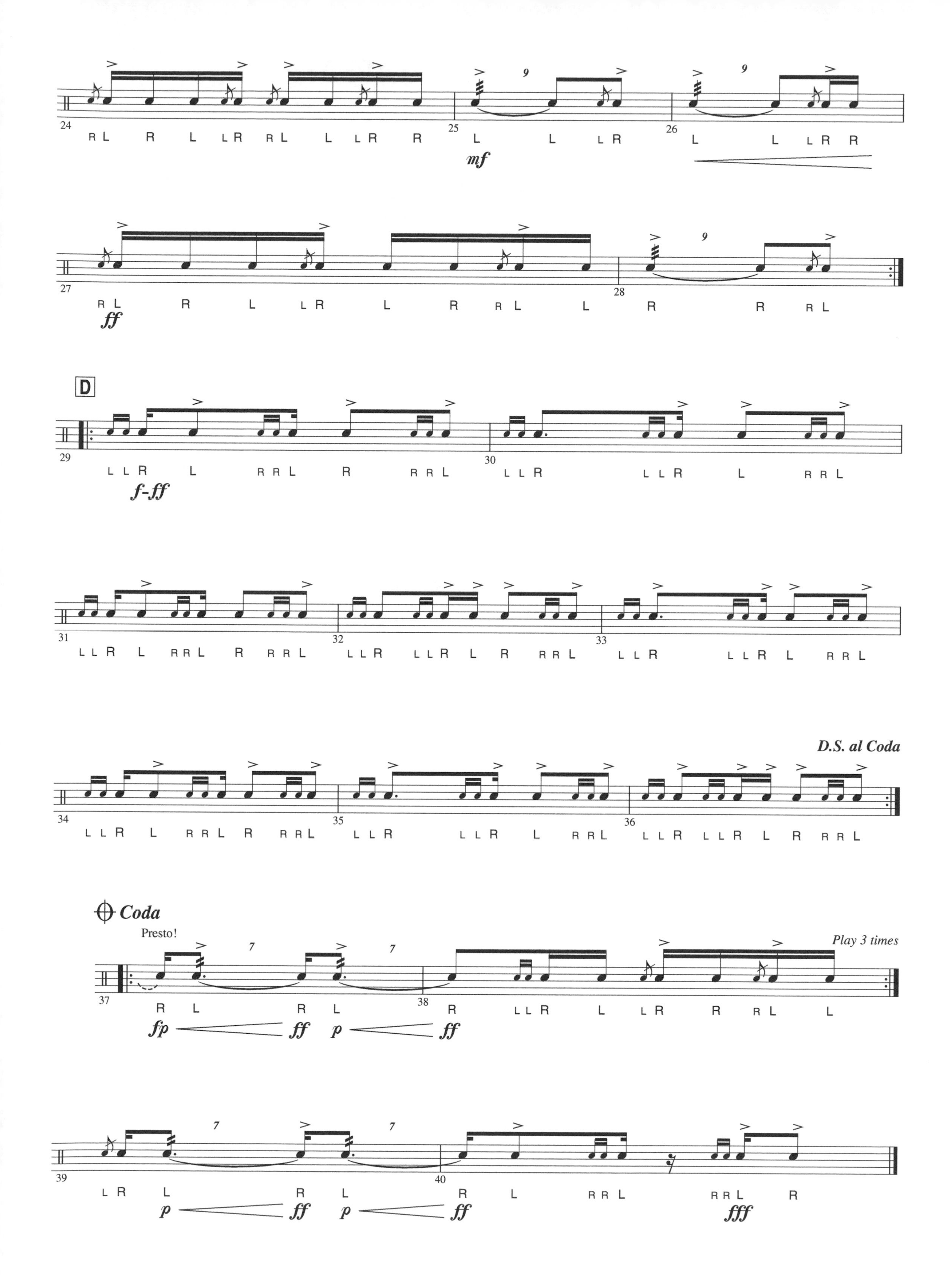

D
D.S. al Coda
Coda
Presto!
Play 3 times

BRIDGE OVER CHESAPEAKE

By BEN HANS

R R R L L L R R R L L R R L
L R LL RR LL RR L R L
R R R L L L R R R L R
R L L R L R L R R L R
R L L R L R L R L L R L R L
R R L R L R L R L R R L R R L L
sfz
E
L R R R L L L R R R L R
mf
R L R L R R R L R
R L L R L R L R R L R R L R L R
L L R L L R L R L R R R L L L R R R L
cresc.
L L R L L R L R L L L R L
R L L R L R L L L R L
R L L R L R L R R L R L R L R L R L
R L R L R L R L R L R L R R L R
molto ritard.
Presto!
sfz

DUSTIN' OFF THE CHOPS

1.
to center
2.
to center
cresc.
ff
C
= 88 In a Dixieland/Swing feel
mp–mf
f
mp
cresc.
to center
ff
D
= 110 a tempo
ff
mf
pp
ff
mp
Tag
cresc.
fff
mp
sffz

FOCUS ON FIVE V

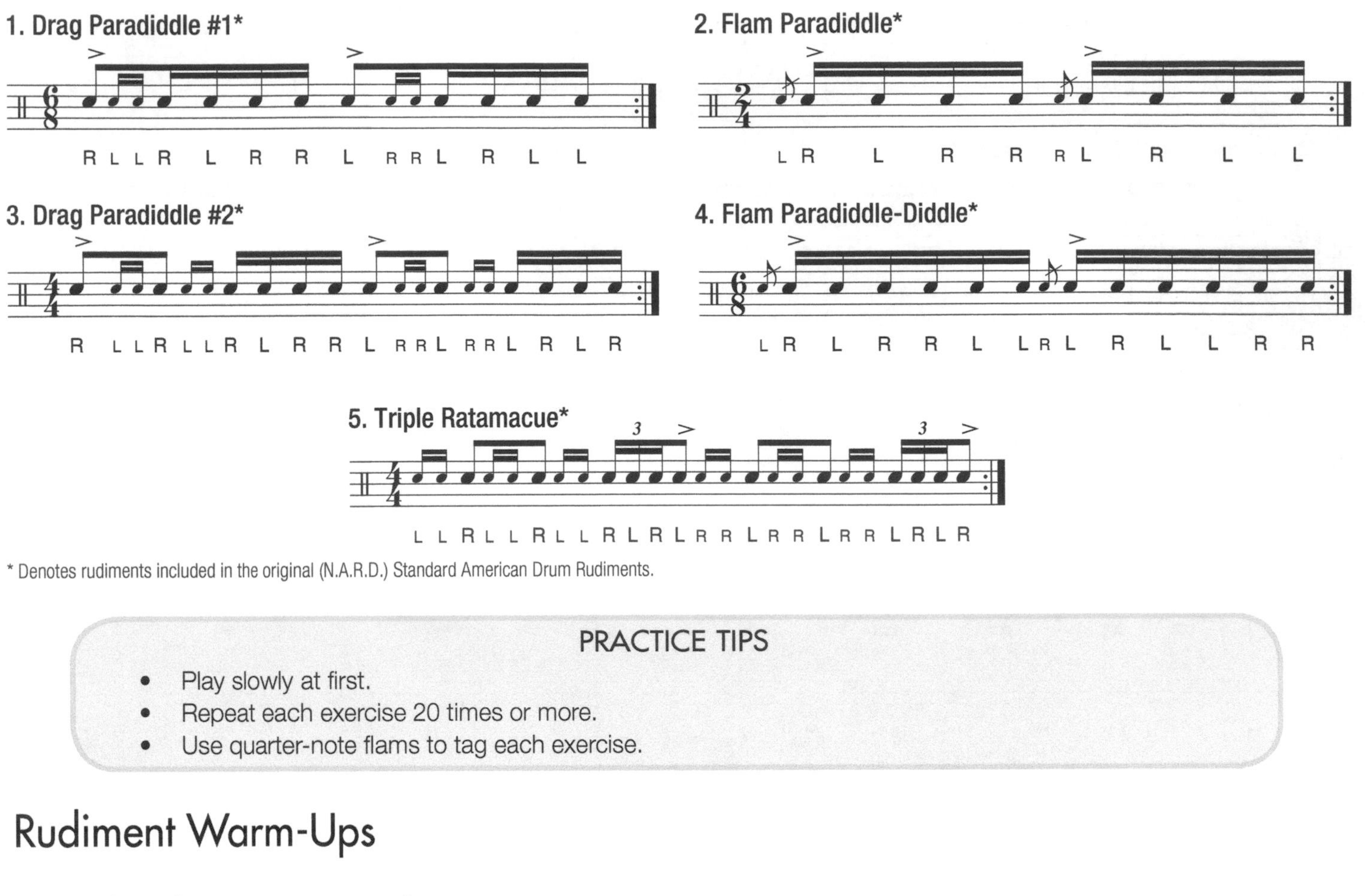

* Denotes rudiments included in the original (N.A.R.D.) Standard American Drum Rudiments.

PRACTICE TIPS

- Play slowly at first.
- Repeat each exercise 20 times or more.
- Use quarter-note flams to tag each exercise.

Rudiment Warm-Ups

STANDING ON THE SHOULDERS OF GIANTS

(Dedicated to John S. "Jack" Pratt and the International Association of Traditional Drummers)

PERFORMANCE TIPS

- Each movement of this solo contains a complete set of the standard 26 (N.A.R.D.) American Drum Rudiments. Can you find them?
- At measure 71–72, build a single stroke roll to your top speed. When finished, proceed to a double stroke roll, and hold until D.S. (no seven stroke roll pickup).
- ⊗ Eleven stroke roll is shown on page 40.

20 L R L R R R L L L R L
21 R L L R L R R L R L L R L R R L R L L R
22 R R L R R L R L R L L R
23 R L L R L R R R L R L R L R R L
24 R
C
25 R R L R L R R L L R L R L
ff
26 L R L R R L L R L R L L R R
27 L R L L R L R R R L R R L R L L
28 L L R L L R L R R L R R L R
29 L L R LL RR LL RR LL RR LL R L R R
30 R L RR LL RR LL RR LL RR L R L L
31 L R L R R L R L L R L L R L R R
mf cresc.
32 R L R L L R L R R L R L L R L R R L R L L
33 L R L R R L R R L L L R L R R L R
34 L L R L R L R L R R R L R L R L R L R L
35 L L R L R R L R L L R L R R L R
36 L L R R R L L L R R R L L L R R R L L
37 RR LL RR LL R L L R R LL RR LL RR L R R L L
38 L R LL RR LL RR LL R R
Play 4 times
39 R L R R L R L L R L R R L R L L R L R R L R L L
accel.
40 R L R L R L R L R L R L R L R

D
♩ = 116
Mvt. II
mf
E
f
fp
cresc.
ff
ritard.
D.S. al Fine
build
f
cresc.

MYLA'S MARCH

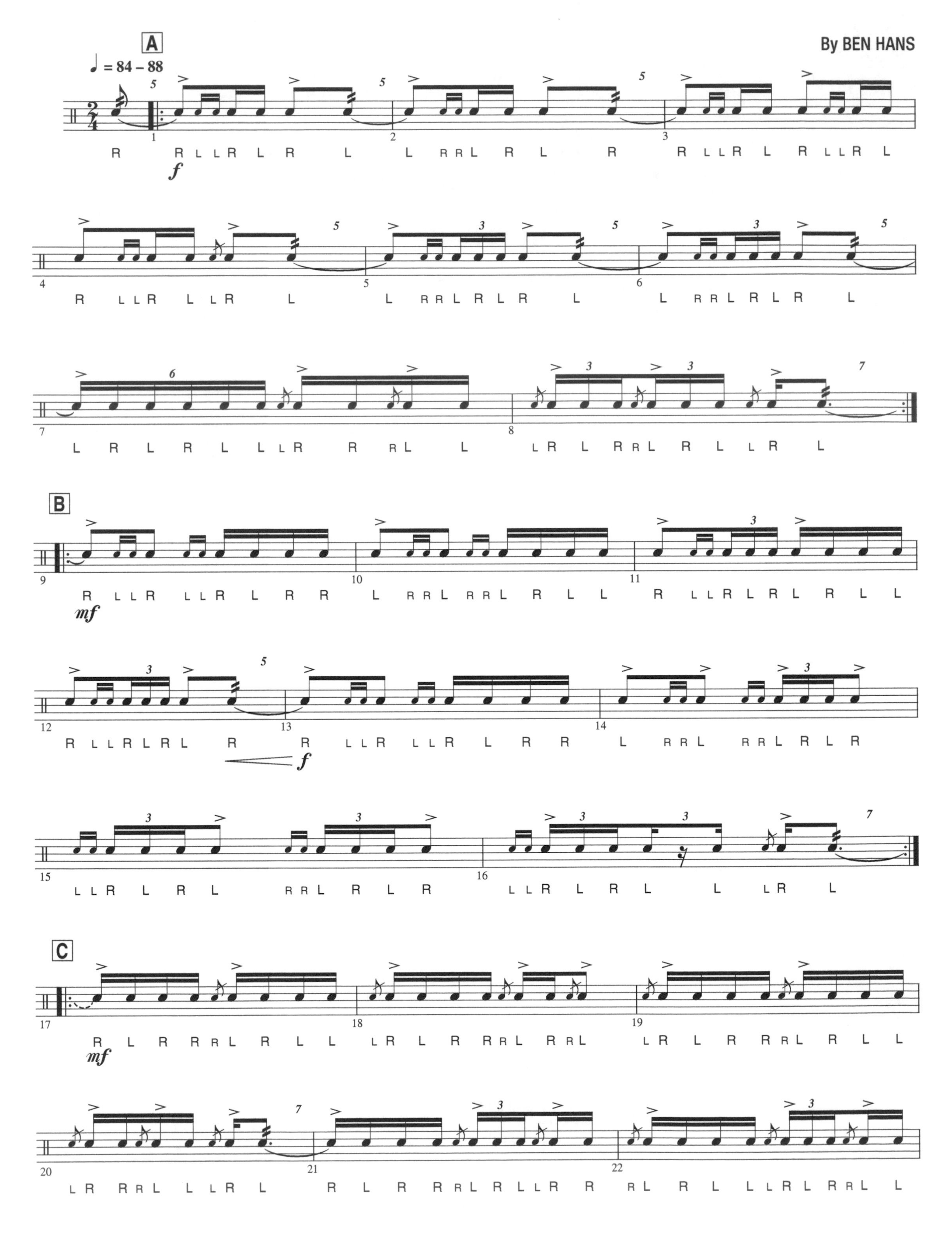

23
L R L R R L L R L R L L R R
24
L R L R R L R R L L R R L
f
D
25
L L R L L R L L R L R L
ff
26
R R L R L R L R L R R L
27
L L R L L R L L R L R L
28
R R L R L R R R L R L R L R R
29
L R R L R R L R L R
30
L L R L L R L L R L R L
31
R R L R R R L R L L R L R R L
32
L L R L R L R L L R R R L
E
Tag
33
L R L R L R L
f
34
R L R L R L R R L
35
L R L R L R R L
36
L L R L R R L R R L L L R L L R L R
37
R L R L R L L R
38
R L R L R L L L R L R R L
39
L L R L R R L R L L R L R R L R L
40
L R L R R L R R L L L R
ff

FOCUS ON FIVE VI

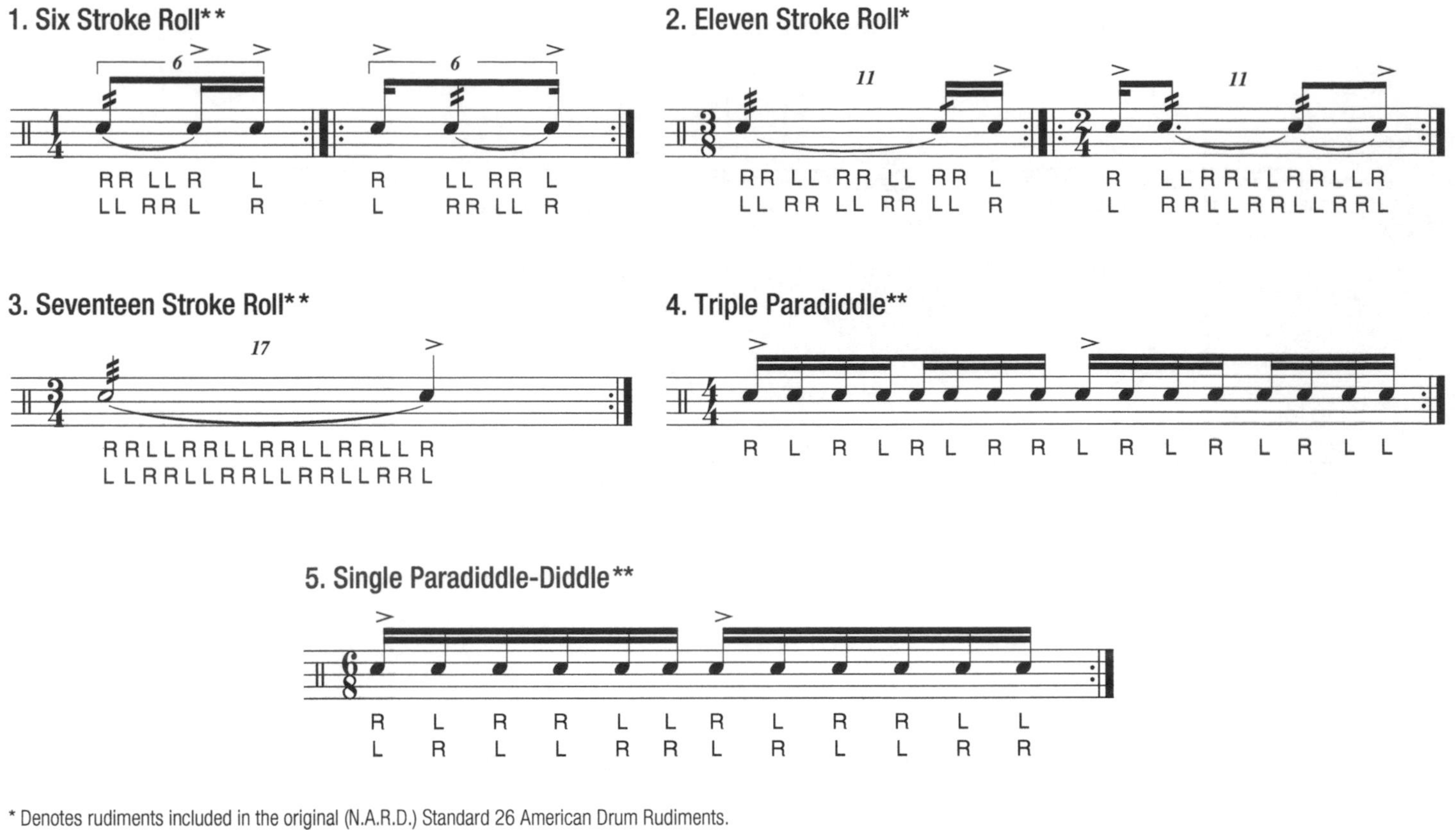

* Denotes rudiments included in the original (N.A.R.D.) Standard 26 American Drum Rudiments.

** Denotes rudiments included in the P.A.S. 40 International Snare Drum Rudiments.

Notes:

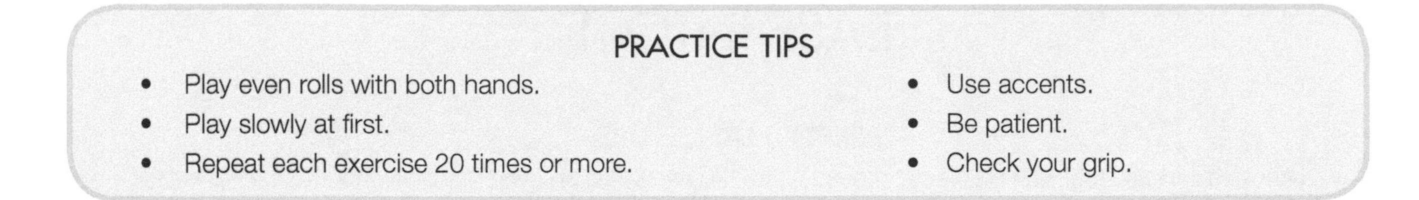

PRACTICE TIPS

- Play even rolls with both hands.
- Play slowly at first.
- Repeat each exercise 20 times or more.
- Use accents.
- Be patient.
- Check your grip.

Rudiment Warm-Ups

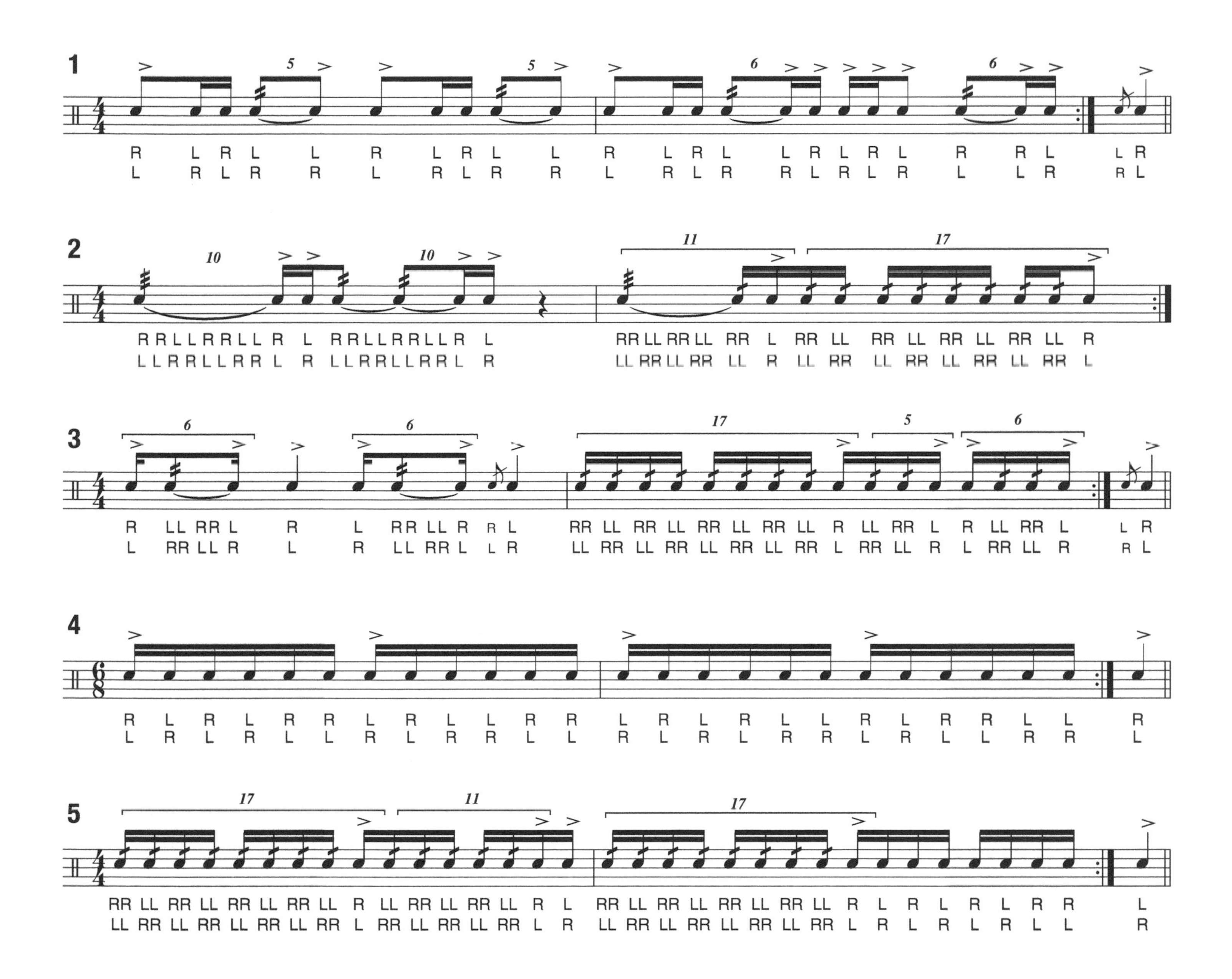

EASE INTO IT

PERFORMANCE TIPS

- Achieve an even feel with diddles at measures 13–20 as well as an even feel of sixteenth notes at letter C.
- Use finger dexterity to assist accents of paradiddle section (letter C).

By BEN HANS

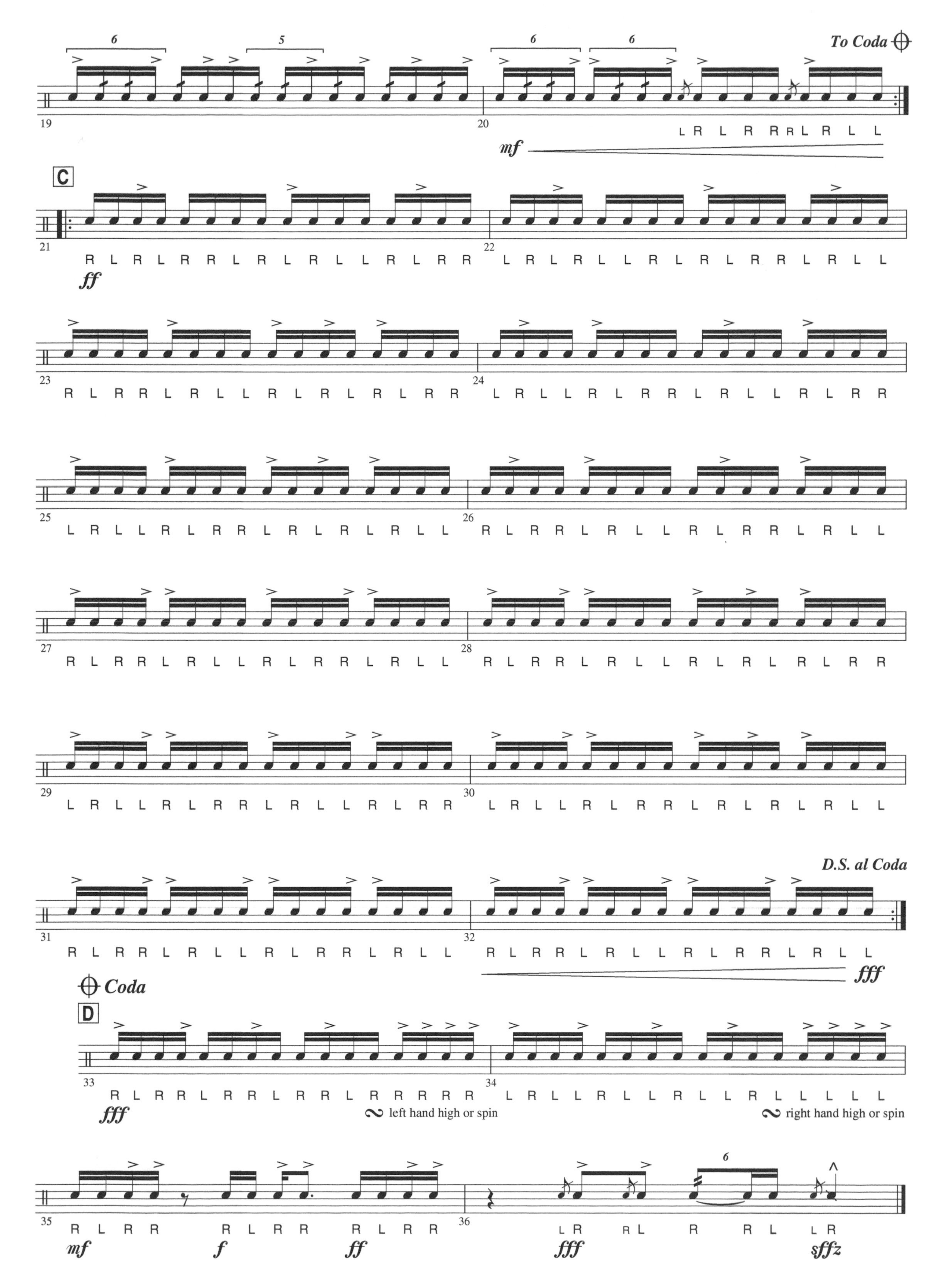
To Coda
19
20
L R L R R R L R L L
mf
C
21
R L R L R R L R L R L L R L R R
22
L R L R L L R L R L R R L R L L
ff
23
R L R R L R L L R L R L R L R R
24
L R L L R L R R L R L L R L R R
25
L R L L R L R R L R L R L R L L
26
R L R R L R L L R L R R L R L L
27
R L R R L R L L R L R R L R L L
28
R L R R L R L L R L R L R L R R
29
L R L L R L R R L R L L R L R R
30
L R L L R L R R L R L R L R L L
D.S. al Coda
31
R L R R L R L L R L R R L R L L
32
R L R R L R L L R L R R L R L L
fff
Coda
D
33
R L R R L R R L R R L R R R R R
34
L R L L R L L R L L R L L L L L
fff
left hand high or spin
right hand high or spin
35
R L R R
R L R R
R L R R
mf
f
ff
36
L R
R L
R
R L
L R
fff
sffz

THE WANDERER

PERFORMANCE TIPS

- Beaming across bar lines is stylistic to rudimental groupings. Correct placement of the beat must be maintained.
- Make sure drags are clean at measures 28 and 31.

By BEN HANS

mf - ff
D
f
sffz
ff
sffz
Fine
mf
sffz
E
mf
mp
f
D.S. al Fine

DOUBLE DRIBBLE DIDDLE

PERFORMANCE TIPS

- Look for the 3:2 son clave beat in letter D. Work this section very slowly at first.
- Hold roll at beginning for at least five or more seconds. Play roll again on D.C.
- Play left hand lead on repeat of A section.
- Do not pause on repeat of D section.

C
D
D.C. al Coda
Coda
Play 5 times
Presto!
to center

FOCUS ON FIVE VII

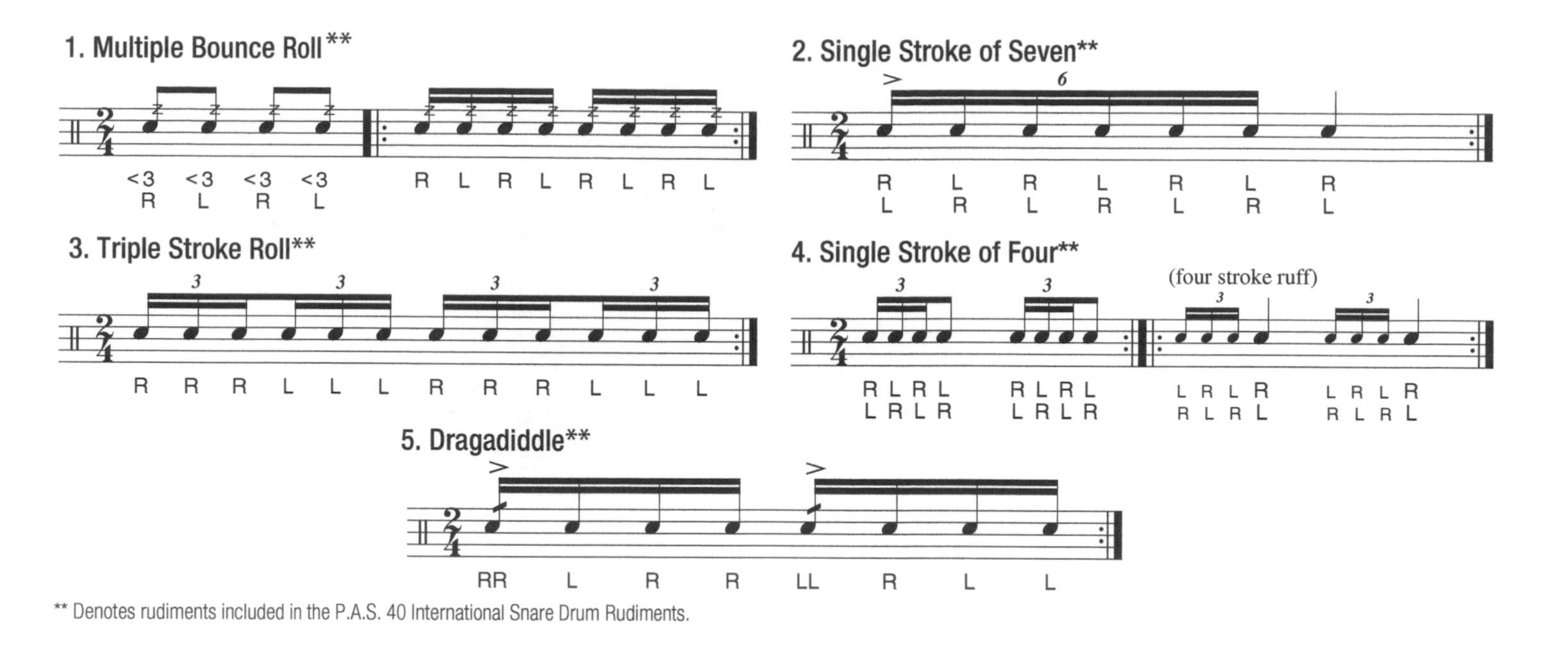

** Denotes rudiments included in the P.A.S. 40 International Snare Drum Rudiments.

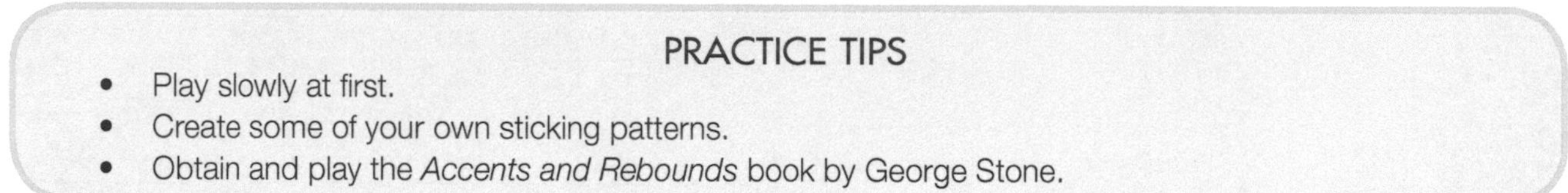

PRACTICE TIPS

- Play slowly at first.
- Create some of your own sticking patterns.
- Obtain and play the *Accents and Rebounds* book by George Stone.

Rudiment Warm-Ups

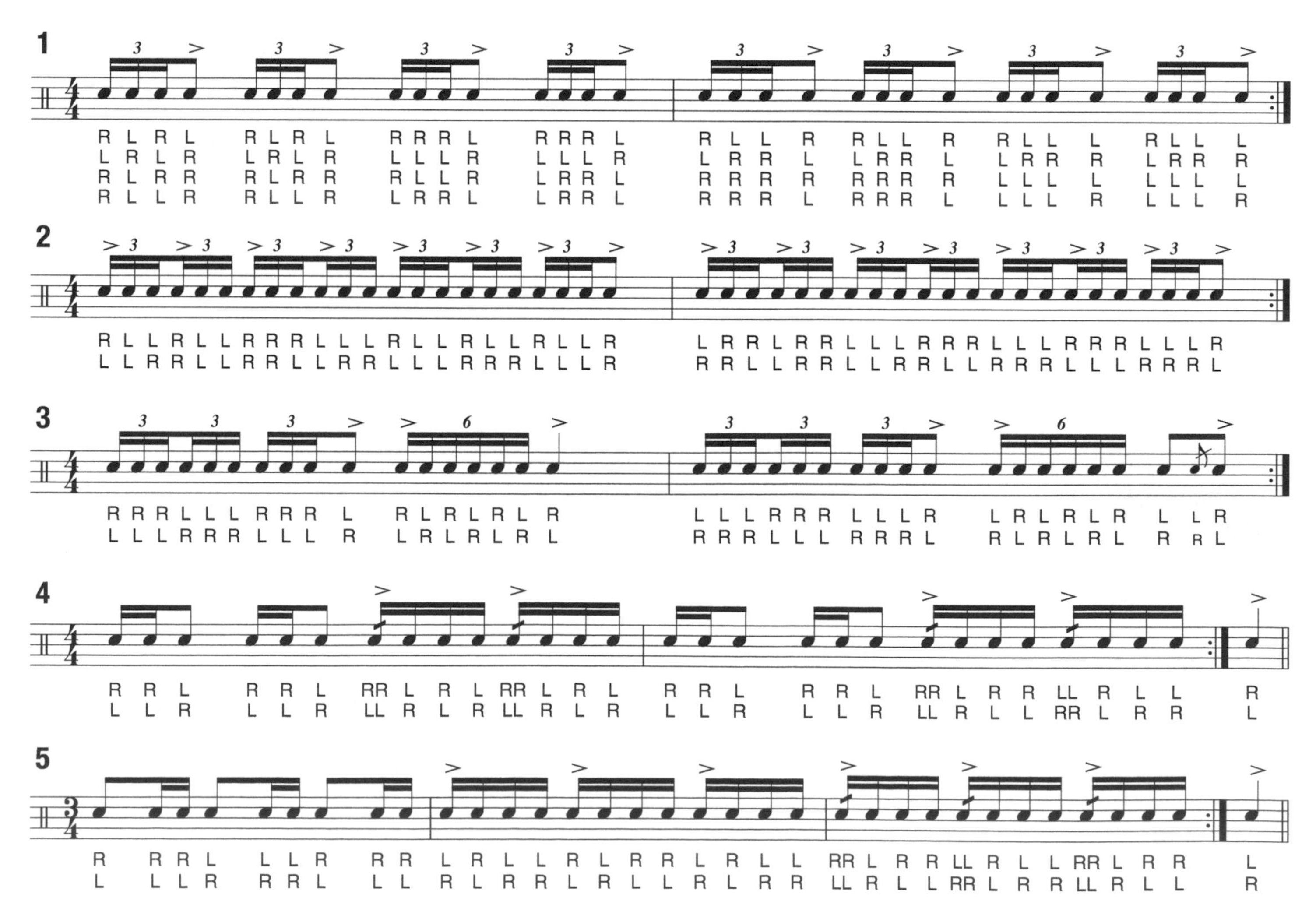

ATOP FORT RODNEY

By BEN HANS

*See the Ratamacue example on page 66.

SAMMIE'S SAMBA

(Dedicated to Samantha Schacht and the West Bend High School Drumline, West Bend, WI)

PERFORMANCE TIPS

- At letter C play side of drum with shaft of right stick to simulate timbale.
- At intro, play both hands together (flat flams or double stops).

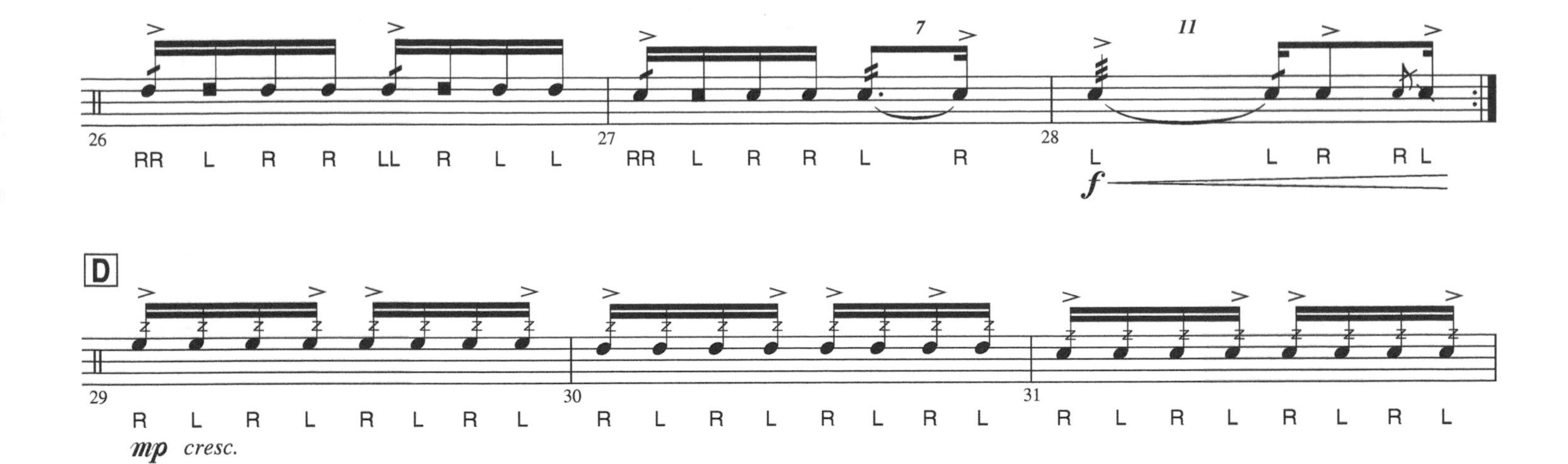
7
11
RR L R R LL R L L
RR L R R L R
L L R R L
f
D
R L R L R L R L
R L R L R L R L
R L R L R L R L
mp cresc.

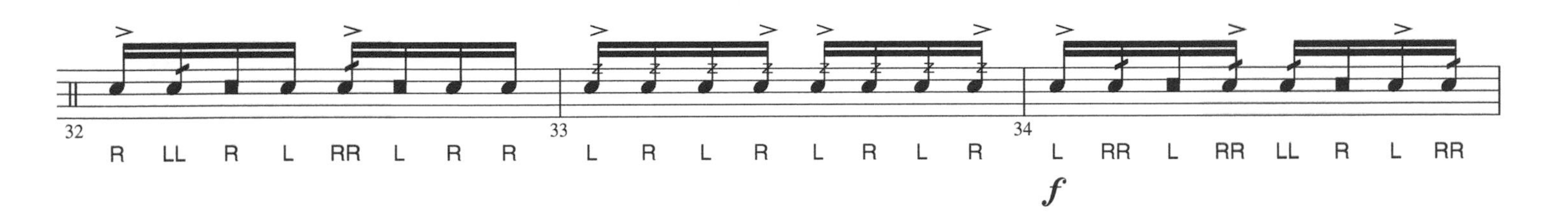
R LL R L RR L R R
L R L R L R L R
L RR L RR LL R L RR
f

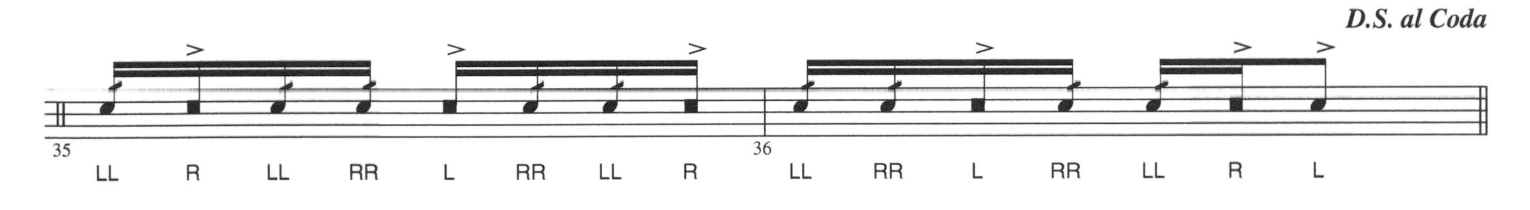
D.S. al Coda
LL R LL RR L RR LL R
LL RR L RR LL R L

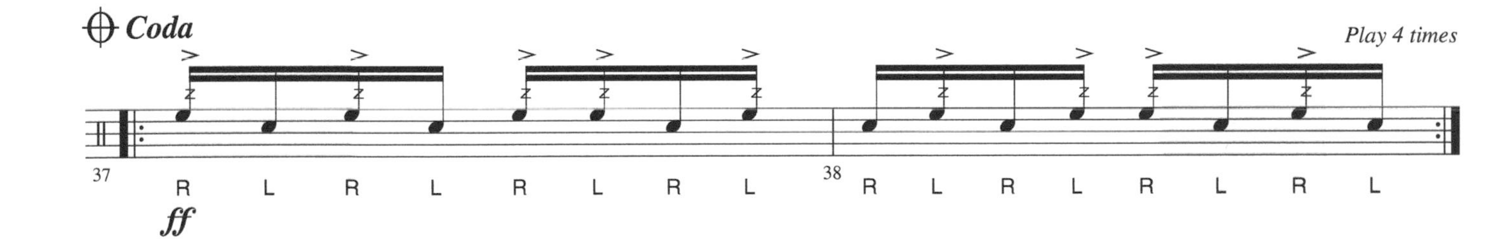
Coda
Play 4 times
R L R L R L R L
R L R L R L R L
ff

6
5
fp
fff
sffz

BEEHIVE

PERFORMANCE TIPS

- Play all strokes cleanly. Practice your triples!
- Play crescendo/decrescendos at will during measure 36.
- Hold rolls at measures 36 and 40 as long as you like.
- Make sure your drags are not crushed.

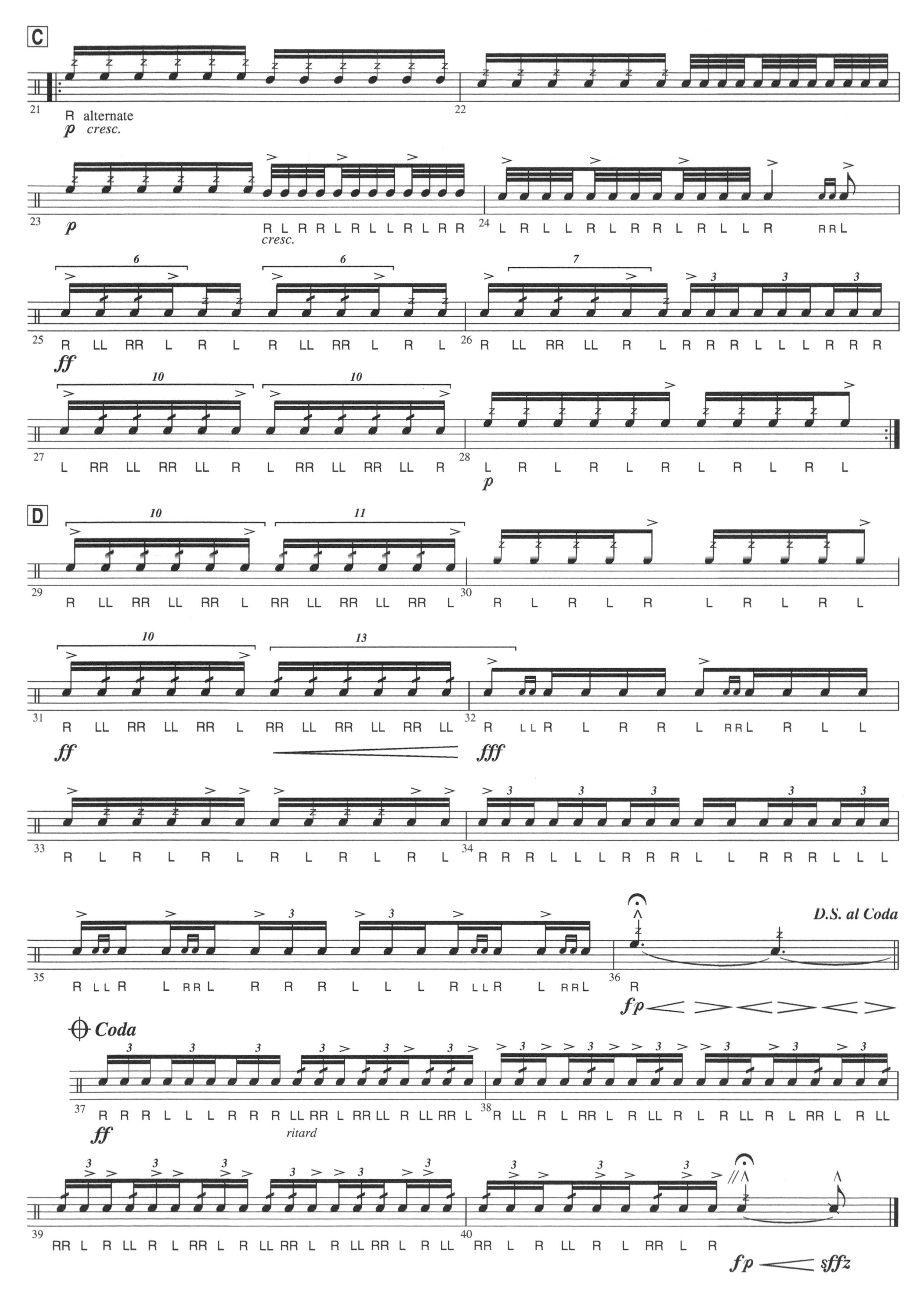
C
R alternate
p cresc.
p
R L R R L R L L R L R R
cresc.
L R L L R L R R L R L L R RRL
R LL RR L R L R LL RR L R L
ff
R LL RR LL R L R R R L L L R R R
L RR LL RR LL R L RR LL RR LL R
L R L R L R L R L R L
p
D
R LL RR LL RR L RR LL RR LL RR L
R L R L R L R L R L
R LL RR LL RR L RR LL RR LL RR LL
R LLR L R R L RRL R L L
ff
fff
R L R L R L R L R L R L
R R R L L L R R R L L R R R L L L
R LLR L RRL R R R L L L R LLR L RRL
R
D.S. al Coda
fp
Coda
R R R L L L R R R LL RR L RR LL R LL RR L
ff
ritard
R LL R L RR L R LL R L R LL R L RR L R LL
RR L R LL R L RR L R LL RR L R LL RR L R LL
RR L R LL R L RR L R
fp
sffz

FOCUS ON FIVE VIII

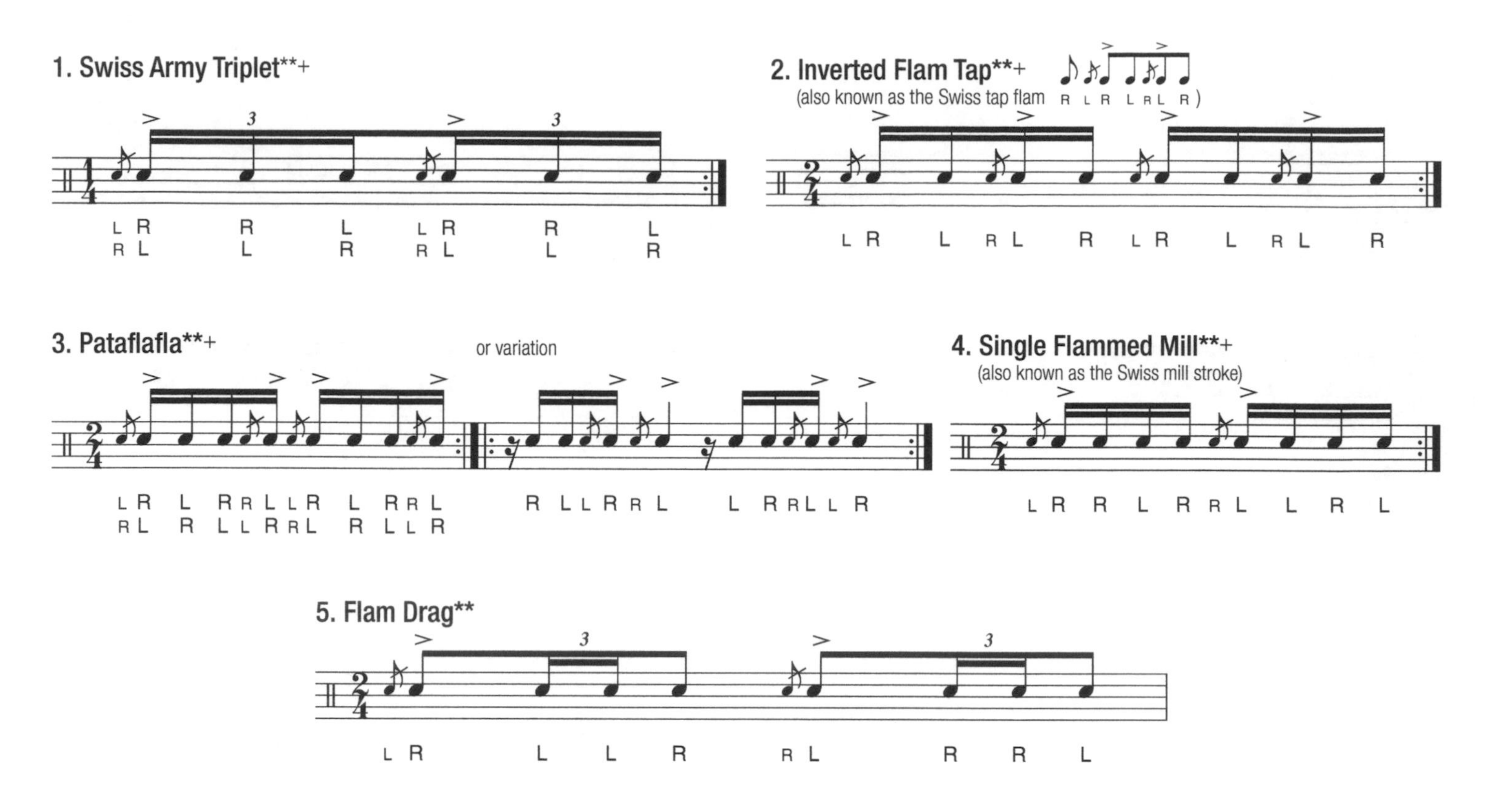

** Denotes rudiments included in the P.A.S. 40 International Snare Drum Rudiments.

+ Denotes Swiss Rudiments.

Notes:

PRACTICE TIPS

- Play slowly at first.
- Play clean flams.
- Play each exercise 20 times or more.
- Read and research Dr. Fritz Berger's book *Instructor for Basle Drumming*.
- Pataflafla rudiment is a Swiss rudiment introduced by the French.
- Research these European rudiments on your own.

Rudiment Warm-Ups

TAMBOR CON CUARENTA EN BOLERO

PERFORMANCE TIPS

- All of the 40 P.A.S. rudiments are contained here. Can you find them?
- Maintain an even and steady 3/4 feel.
- Hold last beat (roll) at your discretion; play closed to open and draw it out dramatically before stopping.

By BEN HANS

C
L L R L R L R R L R L R L L R L R L
L L R L L R L R L R L R R R L R L R
L L R L L R L L R L R L R L R L
R L L R L R LL RR LL RR L R R L
R R R L
R R R L
L L R L R R L R L L R L
mf cresc.
L R R L L R R L L R R L
D
L R L R L R L R L R L R L R R L
ff
L R R L L R L R R L L R R L
R L L R L L R L R R R L L R
LL R L L RR L R R R L L R L
L R L R R L L R L R L L R R L R R L
fff
R L L R L R R L R R L R L L L R R L
R L R L R L R L R L R L R L R L R R L
R R R L L L R R R L L L R L R L
E Tag
R L R L R R L R L R L L L R R L
mf cresc.
R L R R L L R L R R L L R R L
R LL RR L R LL RR L L R R L
to center
R L R L R L R R L R L R L R L L R L
ritard.

SIR LOWERY'S PASS

By BEN HANS

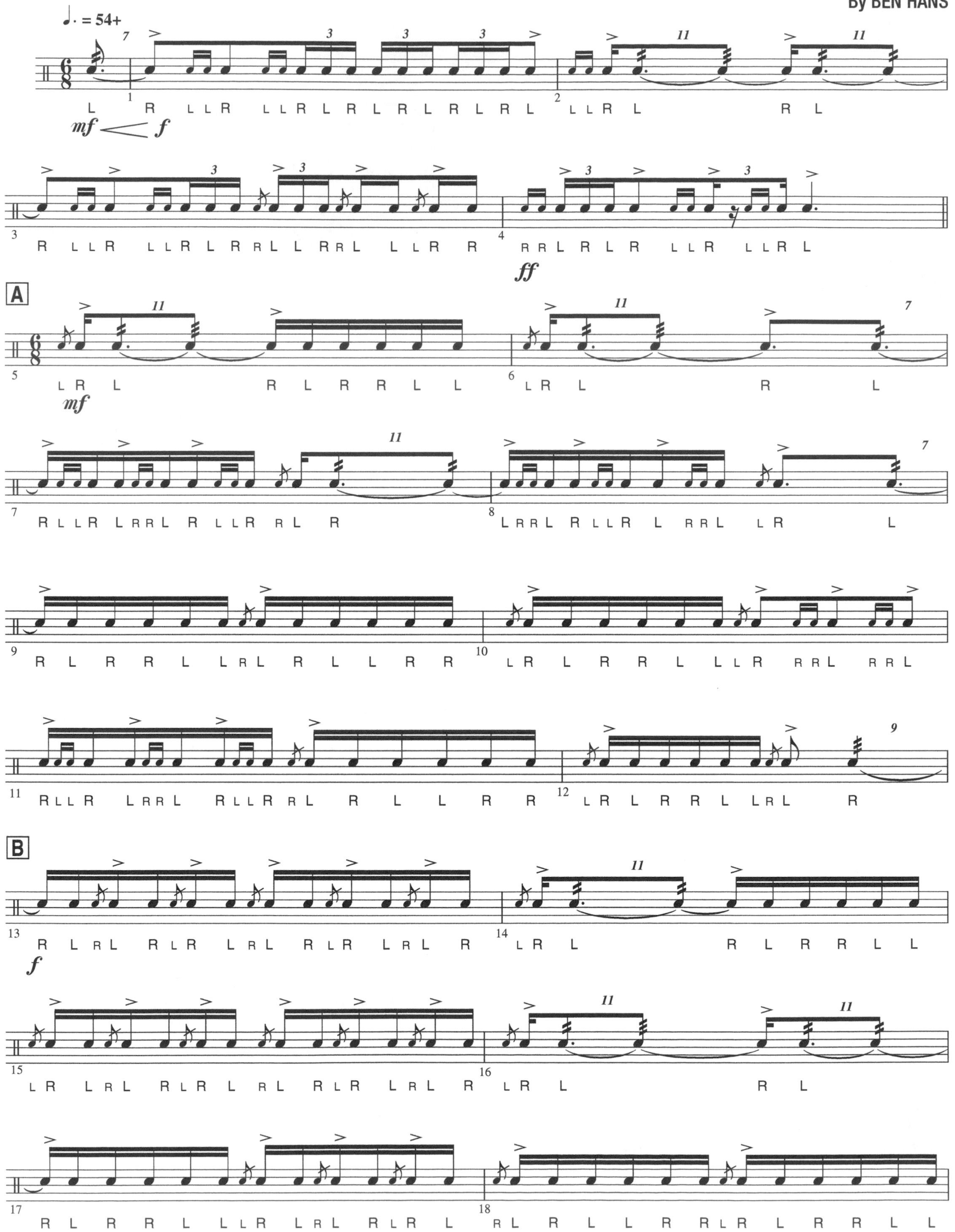

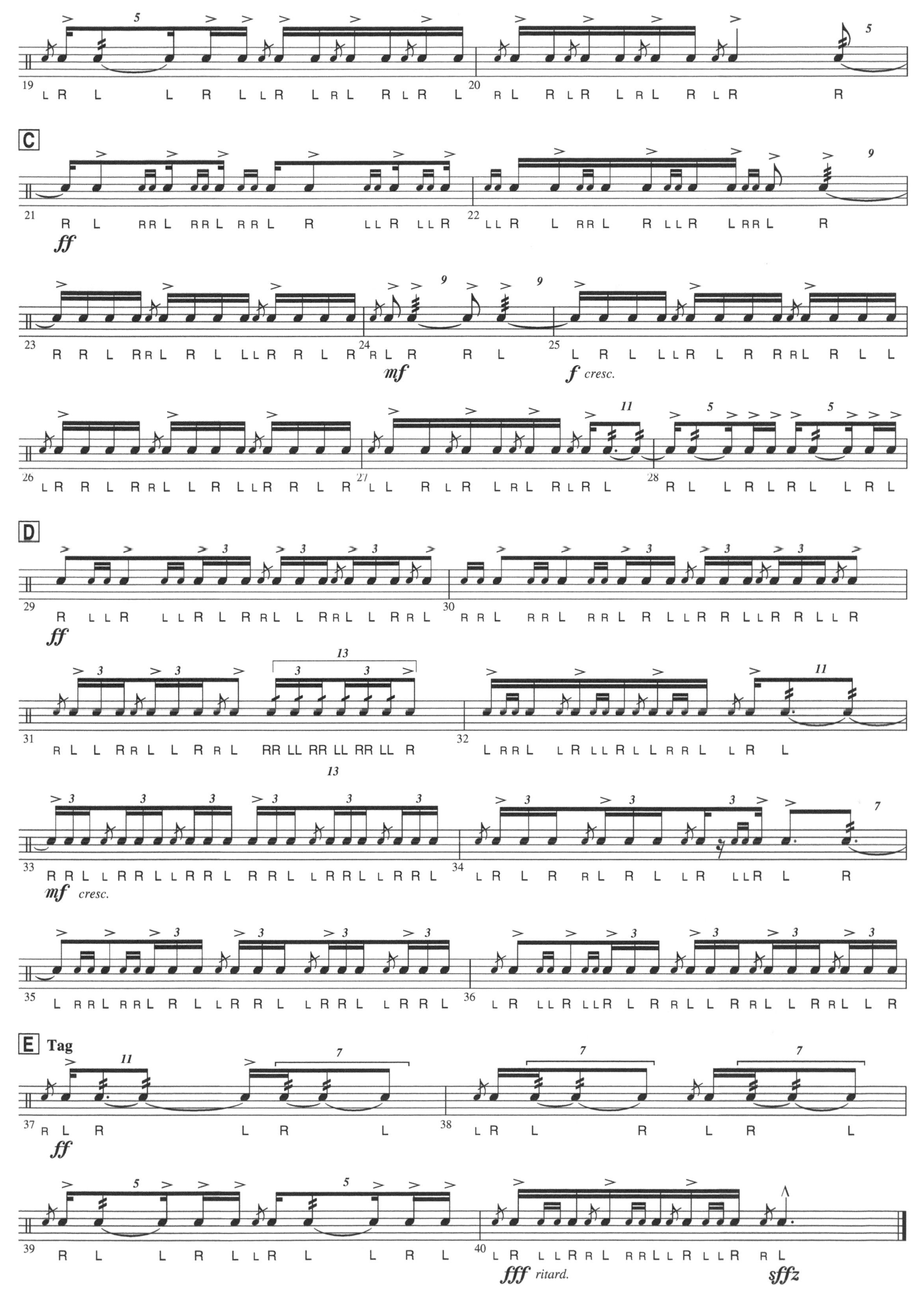
C
ff
mf
f cresc.
D
ff
mf cresc.
E
Tag
ff
fff ritard.
sffz

THE BEACH

(Dedicated to the brave men who landed on the beaches of Normandy on D-Day, June 6th, 1944)

By BEN HANS

Slightly slower
D Juno
1.
2.
E Sword a tempo
accel.
cresc.

FOCUS ON FIVE IX

Hybrid Rudiments (not on the official P.A.S. list)

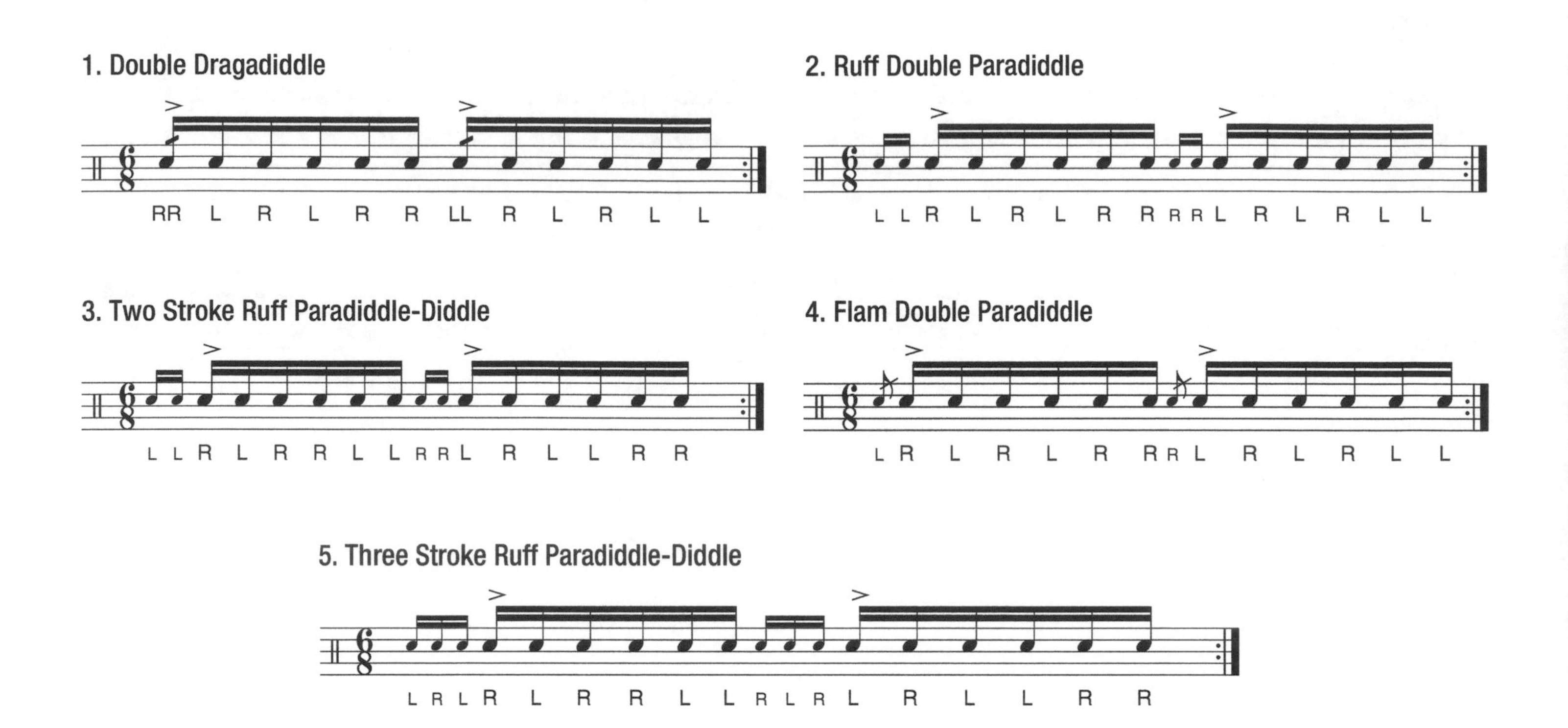

Notes:

PRACTICE TIPS

- Play very slowly at first. DO NOT RUSH!
- Be very aware of your sticking.
- Be sure to learn to phrase grace notes before the beat.
- Feel the difference between on the beat and before the beat regarding grace notes.

Rudiment Warm-Ups

QUEEN ANNE'S REVENGE

By BEN HANS

C
21
R L R L R R RRL R L R L L
22
LLR L R L R R L L
23
LLR L R R L LRRL R L L R R
24
LLR LL RR L RR LLR RL R L
25
LR RL R LLR RL LR L RRL
26
LR R LLR R LLR R LLR RL L RRL
f
27
LR R LLR R LLR RL L RRL L RRL
mf
28
LR LL RR LL RR L RRL R LLR LL
ff
D
29
R LLR L R L RRL RRL R L R
30
LL R L R L L RR L R R L
31
LR L R L R RRL R L R L L
32
LR LRL RLL RRL R L R L L
33
R LLR L R L LRLR L R R L L RLRL R L
poco ritenuto
34
L R RLRLR L R R L LRL R L L R RLR
35
RL RRL R L R RLRL R L L R R L
36
LRLR RLRL LRLR RLRL R L L R RLRLR L R
E Tag
37
R L L RLRL R L L R R LRLR L R R L LLR R L
38
LR R LLR R LLR R LLR R L LR R L L R
sffz
39
RLRL R L L R R L LRLR L R R L L
mf cresc.
40
R RLRL R L L R R L LR
ff

FOCUS ON FIVE X

Swiss and Hybrid Rudiments (not on the official P.A.S. list)

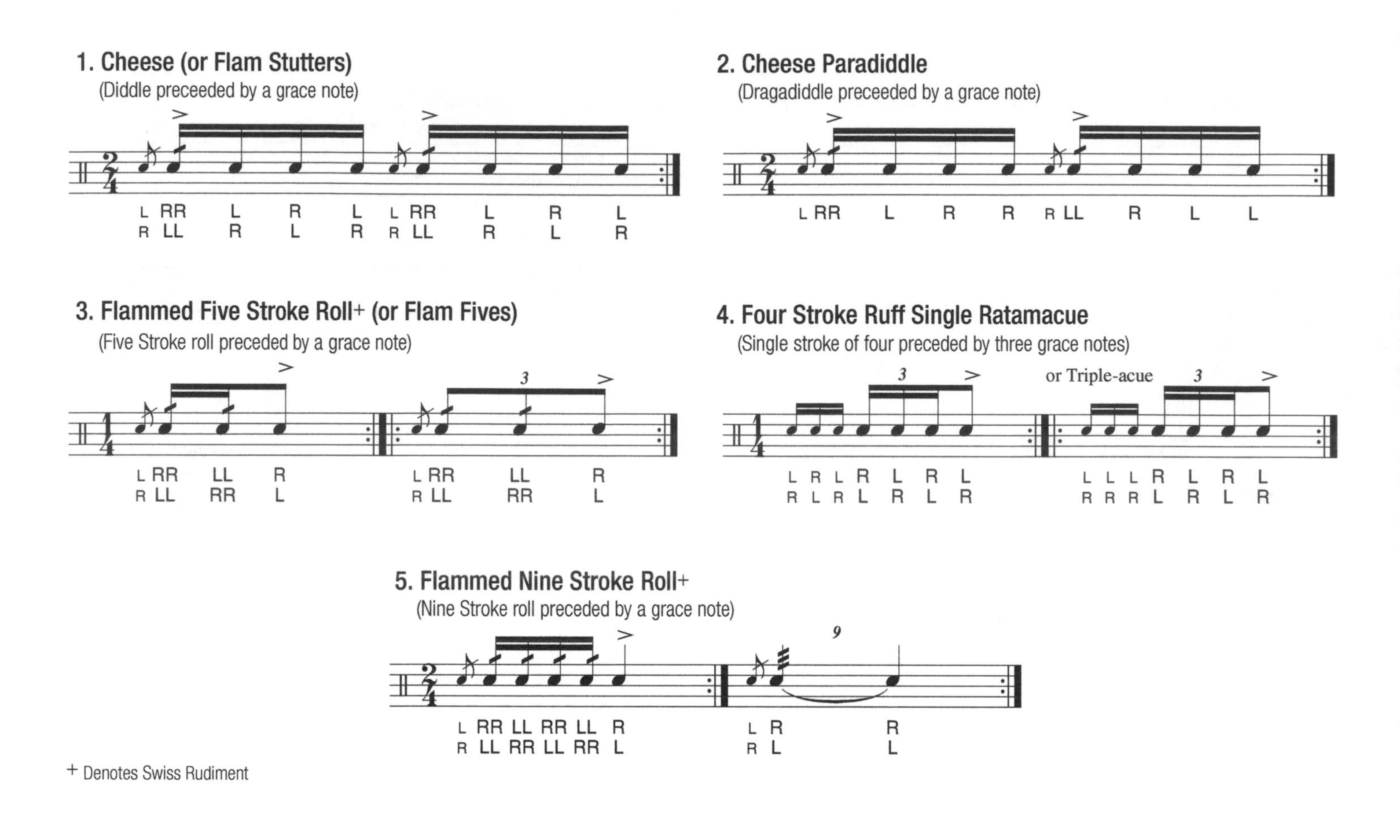

+ Denotes Swiss Rudiment

Notes:

PRACTICE TIPS

- Play slowly and cleanly, then work up your tempo.
- Dr. Fritz Berger's *Instructor for Basle Drumming* instructs the Flammed Five Stroke, Flammed Nine Stroke, and Swiss Army Triplets as "one-way drum figures" with a right-hand lead only.
- Dr. John Wooten calls rudiment 1 "Flam Stutters" in his book *The Drummer's Rudimental Reference Book*, p. 101. This figure can also be compared to Dr. Fritz Berger's "Flammed Three Stroke Roll" on p. 24 of his book *Instructor for Basle Drumming*.
- Call them whatever you want, but play them correctly.
- Research these Swiss rudiments on your own.

Rudiment Warm-Ups

BUCKY WAGON

(Dedicated to Mitchell Luangrath of the University of Wisconsin - Madison Snare Drum Line)

22 L R R L R 23 R L R R R LL R L L 24 L RR L R R R LL R L L
f
25 L RR L L RR L L R R L R 26 R L L 27 R L L L R R L
1. 2.
mf ff
D
28 L R R R LL R R L 29 L R R L L RR L 30 L R R R L L R R L
f - ff
31 L R R L L R R L L RR L R R 32 R L L L RR L L R
33 R L L L RR LL R 34 R LL R L L L RR L L R R L
1. 2.
35 L R R L L R R L L R R LL R R L 36 L R R L L R R L L R R L L R R L
E Tag
Presto!
37 L R R R L L R 38 L R R R L L R R L 39 L RR LL R R LL RR L L RR LL
fff
40 R R LL RR L L R 41 R R L L R R L L RR LL RR L

FOCUS ON FIVE XI

Hybrid Rudiments (not on the official P.A.S. list)

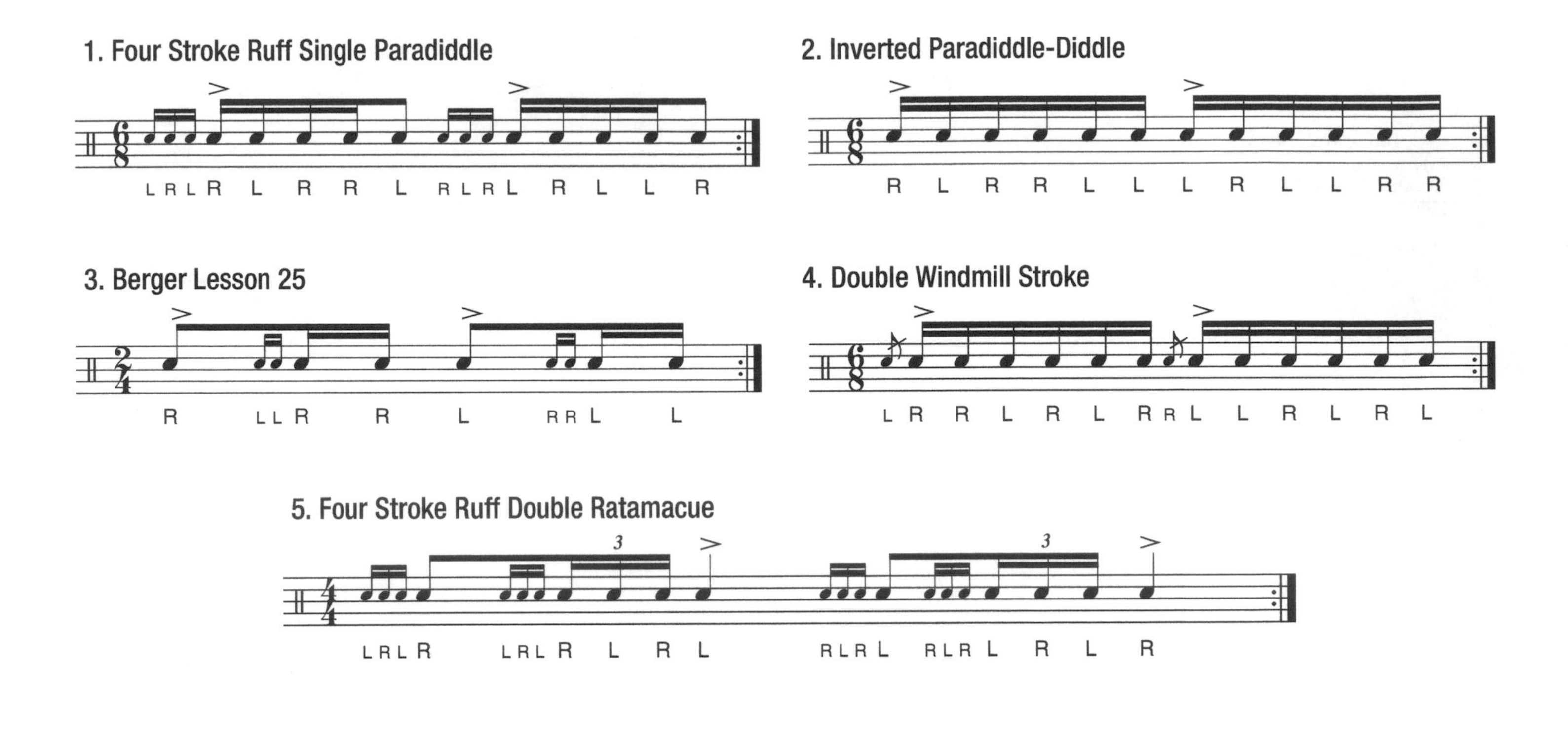

Notes:

PRACTICE TIPS

- Play all rudiments at a slow pace to learn correct sticking.
- Learn the difference between the triplet on the beat and the three grace notes before the beat.
- Rudiment 3 has been associated with Dr. Fritz Berger from his solo "Rudimenter Good Luck," on p. 59 of the book *America's N.A.R.D. Drum Solos*. However, its roots are not of Swiss origin but of French origin. See Allen C. Benson's "Readers Response" article in the Percussive Notes Research Edition, *Percussionist*, Vol. 18, No. 2, Winter 1981, page 2.

Rudiment Warm-Ups

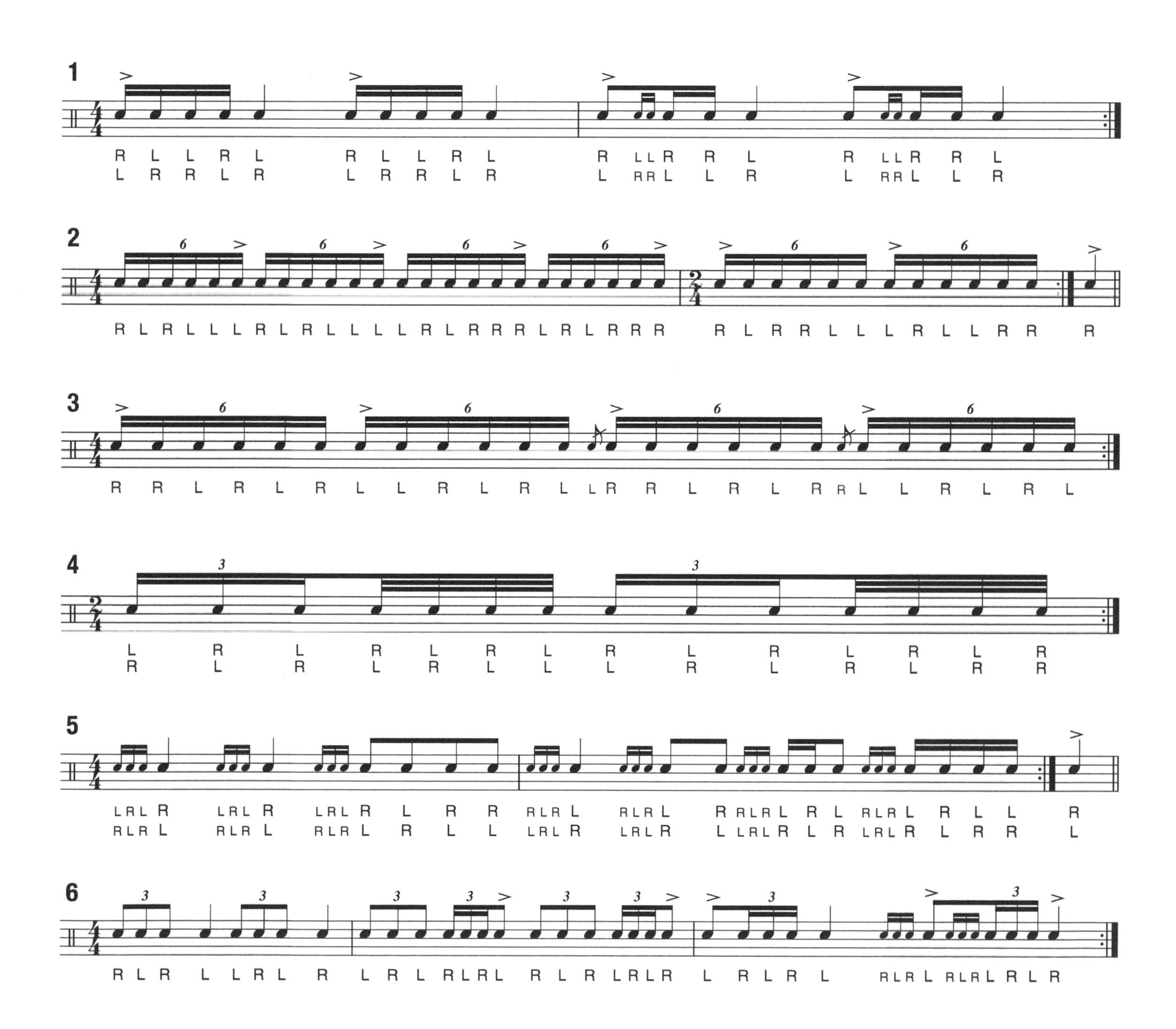

E-GAD, INVERTED PARADIDDLE-DIDDLES!?

PERFORMANCE TIPS

- Perform roll "closed to open" at start.
- Draw out letter B as slowly as you like.
- Play close attention to sticking throughout.
- Take a very short pause at the end of your roll in measure 16 before continuing.

By BEN HANS

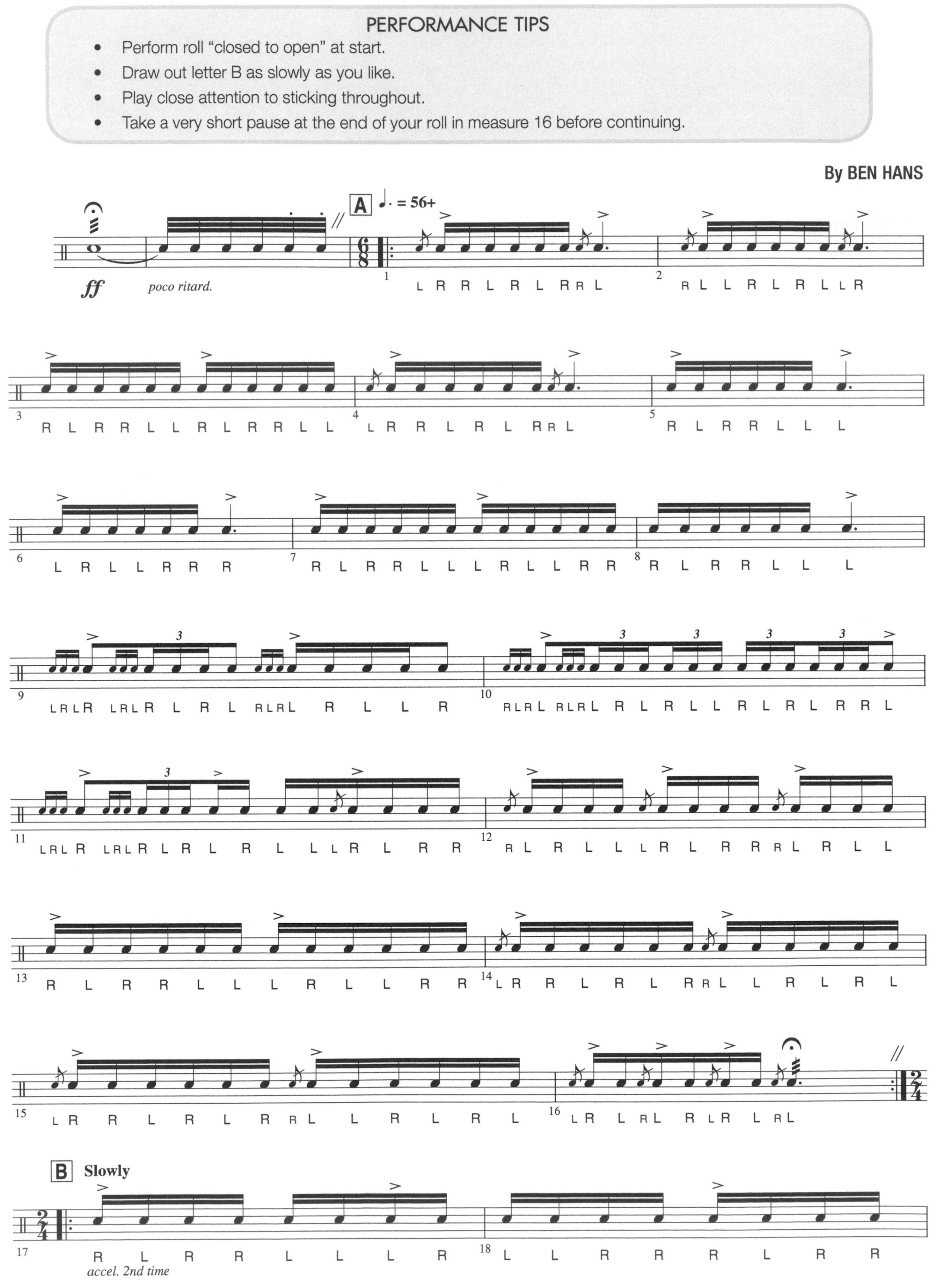

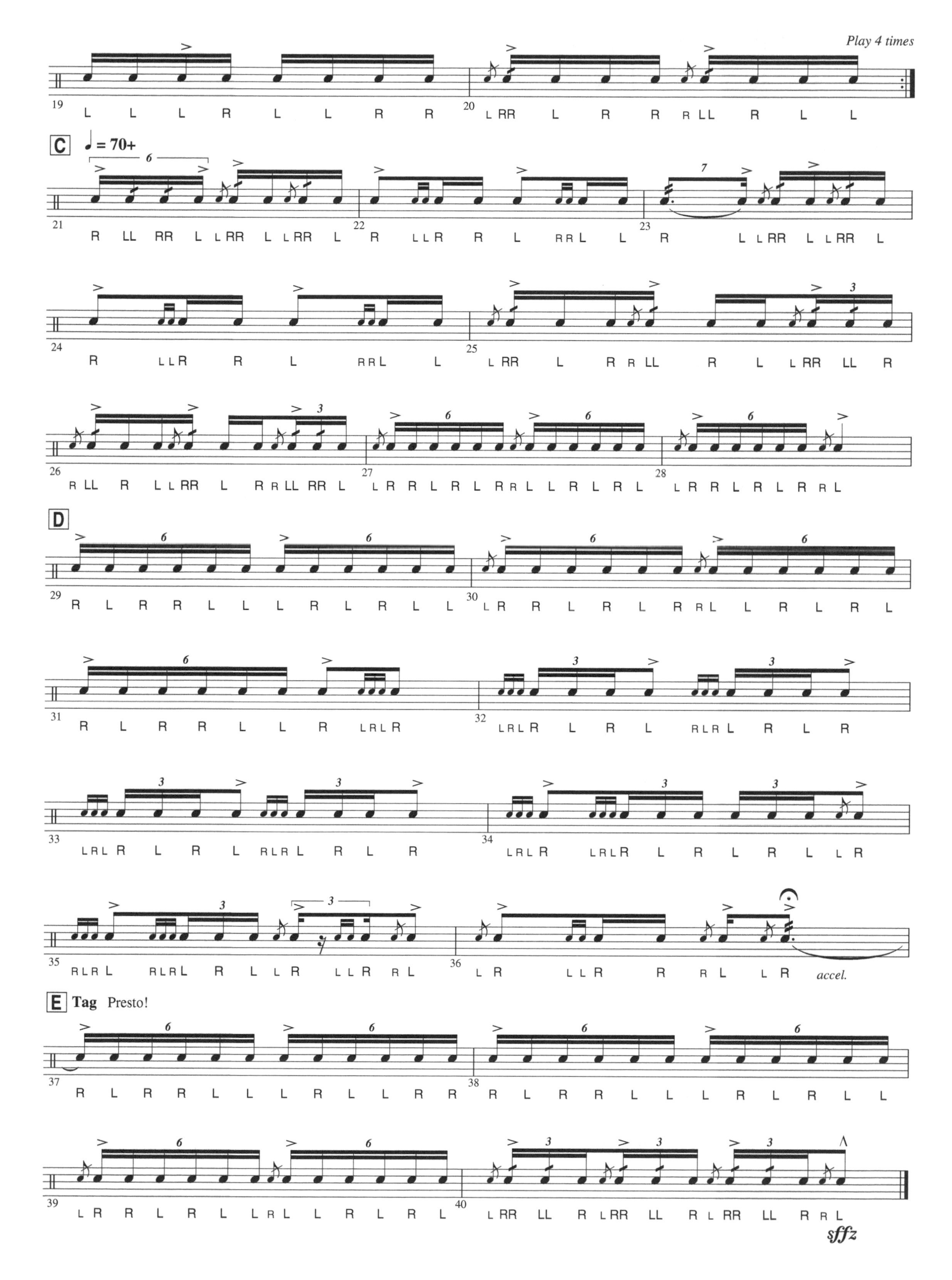
Play 4 times
C
= 70+
D
accel.
E Tag Presto!
sffz

SELECT BIBLIOGRAPHY

Suggested Reference and Solo Materials

For a more comprehensive and continually updated listing, check out the rudimental page at **www.benhans.com**.

Berger, Dr. Fritz R. *Instructor for Basle Drumming*. Basle, Switzerland: Trommelverlag, 1937.

Campbell, James. *Rudiments in Rhythm*. Galesville, MD: Meredith Music, 2002.

Cook, Gary D. *Teaching Percussion*. Belmont, CA: Thomson Schirmer, 2006.

Combs, F. Michael. *Percussion Manual, 2nd Edition*. Prospect Heights, CA: Waveland Press, 2000.

Cuccia, Dominick. *The Beat of A Different Drummer.* Galesville, MD: Meredith Music, 2004.

Freytag, Edward, et al. *Just Desserts, the Rudimental Cookbook Volume II*. Nashville, TN: Row-Loff Publications, 2001.

Freytag, Edward, et al. *The Rudimental Cookbook*. Nashville, TN: Row-Loff Productions, 1993.

Ludwig, William F., et al. *National Association of Rudimental Drummers N.A.R.D. Drum Solos*. Chicago, IL: Ludwig Drum Co., 1962.

McCormick, Larry W. *Precision Drumming: The McCormick Method*. Elgin, IL: Percussion Enterprises, 1965.

Moeller, Sanford A. *The Art of Snare Drumming*. Cleveland, OH: Ludwig Drum Co., 1950.

Moore, J. Burns. *The Art of Drumming*. Chicago, IL: Ludwig Drum Co., 1937.

Mott, Vincent L. *Evolution of Drumming*. Paterson, NJ: Music Textbook Company, 1957.

Pratt, John S. *14 Modern Contest Solos for Snare Drum*. Miami, FL: Alfred/WB (CCP/Belwin) Publishing, 1959.

Pratt, John S. *The New Pratt Book*. Columbus, OH: Permus Publications, 1985.

Pratt, John S. *Rudimental Solos for Accomplished Drummers*. Galesville, MD: Meredith Music Publishers, 2000.

Pratt, John S., William J. Schinstine and James L. Moore. *The Solo Snare Drummer*. Columbus OH: Permus Publications, 1985.

Queen, Jeff. *The Next Level: Rudimental Snare Technique*. Plano, TX: Mark Wessels Publications, 2004.

Rich, Buddy and Henry Adler. *Buddy Rich's Modern Interpretation of Snare Drum Rudiments*. New York, NY: Embassy Music/Music Sales Corp., 1942.

Stone, George Lawrence. *Accents and Rebounds*. Randolph, MA: George B. Stone & Son, 1961.

Stone, George Lawrence. *Stick Control*. Randolph, MA: George B. Stone & Son, 1935.

Sylvia, Neil, et al. *Ziggadabuzz*. Nashville, TN: Row-Loff Productions, 2001.

Tilles, Bob. *Reading Exercises for Snare Drum*. Chicago, IL: G.I.A. Publications, 1971.

Wanamaker, Jay and Rob Carson. *Percussive Arts Society Official International Drum Rudiments*. Van Nuys, CA: Alfred Publishing, 1984.

Wanamaker, Jay A. *Corps Style Snare Drum Dictionary*. VanNuys, CA: Alfred Publishing, 1981.

Wilcoxson, Charley. *The All American Drummer*. Cleveland, OH: Ludwig Music Publishing, 1945.

Wilcoxson, Charley. *Modern Rudimental Swing Solos for the Advanced Drummer*. Cleveland, OH: Ludwig Music Publishing, 1941.

Wooten, John. *The Drummer's Rudimental Reference Book*. Nashville, TN: Row-Loff Productions, 1992.

Video and Audio Recordings

The following recordings and videos are suggested for study:

Arsenault, Frank. *The 26 Standard American Drum Rudiments*. LP, Ludwig Recording, 1955.

Beecher, Mark. *The Art of Ancient Rudimental Drumming*. DVD, Mark Beecher Production, www.markbeecher.com, 1996.

Gauthreaux, Guy G. II. *Open-Close-Open American Contest Solos for Snare Drum*. CD, Pioneer Percussion, 1999.

Gauthreaux, Guy G. II. *Rudiments, Rudiments, Rudiments!* 40 International Snare Drum Rudiments and six graded snare drum solos. CD, Pioneer Percussion, 2004.

The Historic Drummer's Heritage Concert at the Percussive Arts Society International Convention 2002. DVD, Percussive Arts Society: Indianapolis, IN, 2002.

Reference Articles

The following articles can be obtained through the Percussive Arts Society website archives, from past editions of *Percussive Notes*, and the *Percussionist* publications. www.pas.org (You must join as a PAS member to access these articles.)

Benson, Allen C. "An Introduction to the Swiss Rudiments and Their Notation." *Percussionist*: Vol. 17, No. 3, Spring/Summer, 1980: 140–148.

Donnelly, Jeff. "On the Technical Side, Swiss Rudiments." *Percussive Notes*: Vol. 16, No. 2, Winter, 1978: 52–53.

Fink, Ron. "The 42 Standard Rudiments? To Revise or Not Revise." *Percussive Notes*: Vol. 10, No. 2, Winter, 1972: 12–14.

Galm, John K. "A Study of the Rudiments Used in Foreign Military Drumming Styles." *Percussionist*: February, 1965: Vol. 2, Nos. 1 and 2. (Corrections appear in *Percussionist*, 1967.)

Hartsough, Jeff and Derrick Logozzo. "The Timeline of Marching and Field Percussion: Parts 1–4." *Percussive Notes*: August, 1994: 48–52. October, 1994: 20–24. December, 1994: 30–33. February, 1995: 26–35.

Ludwig, William F., et al. "What to Do With the Rudiments." *Percussive Notes*: Vol. 10, 1972: 16–18.

Mazur, Ken. "The Perfectionists, The History of Rudimental Snare Drumming from Military Code to Field Competition." *Percussive Notes*: April, 2005: 10–21.

McGrath, William A. "The Contribution of Senior Drum and Bugle Corps to Marching Percussion." *Percussionist*: Vol. 17, No. 3, Spring/Summer 1980: 149–175.

McInnis, Fred. "The History of the 40 international Snare Drum Rudiments." *Percussive Notes*: April, 2005: 24–28.

Salmon, James D. "Percussion Education Department." *Percussionist*: Vol. 3, Nos. 2 and 3, April, 1966: 39–41.

Smales, Joel. "Hybrid Snare Drum Rudiments." *Percussive Notes*: April, 2005: 30–39.

Spalding, Dan C. "The Evolution of Drum Corps Drumming." *Percussionist*: Vol. 17, No. 3, Spring/Summer, 1980: 116–131.

Spaulding, Dan C. "Drag Interpretation for the Rudimental Drummer." *Percussive Notes*: April, 1985: 61–62.

Wanamaker, Jay, and the PAS Marching Percussion Committee. "PAS International Drum Rudiment Proposal." *Percussive Notes*: October, 1982: 74–77.

Wyman, Chad. "Teaching Compound Rudiments Through Basics." *Percussive Notes*: December, 1997: 26–28.

GLOSSARY

Music Terms and Articulations Used in This Book

TERMS

accelerando	gradually faster
a tempo	return to original tempo or rate of speed
crescendo	< gradually louder
decrescendo	> gradually softer
largo	slow
molto	much; very
poco	little
presto	fast; rapid
ritardando (ritard.)	gradually slower
ritenuto	held back; at a slower rate of speed.
rubato	stolen time – allows for a speeding up and/or slowing down at the interpretation of the performer.
simile	continue in the same manner, style

ARTICULATIONS

>	accent	play note with strong attack
∧	marcato	loud, emphasized accent
·	staccato	short, detached
𝄐	fermata	hold out
//	break (caesura or railroad tracks)	short pause

DYNAMICS

ppp	pianississimo	very, very soft
pp	pianissimo	very soft
p	piano	soft
mp	mezzo piano	moderately soft
mf	mezzo forte	moderately loud
f	forte	loud
ff	fortissimo	very loud
fff	fortississimo	very very loud
sfz	sforzando	special stress and sudden emphasis
sffz	sforzatiffimo	perform with sudden emphasis at a very loud volume
fp	forte piano	loud, soft

mf–f mezzo forte on first time through, forte on second time through

REPEAT TERMS AND SIGNS

D.C. (Da Capo)	return to the beginning
D.S. (Dal Segno)	return to the sign (𝄋)
𝄋	section repeat sign (segno)
𝄌	coda sign, ending of an arrangement
D.C. al Fine	da capo, return to beginning, play to Fine
D.S. al Fine	dal segno, return to the sign (𝄋), play to Fine
D.C. al Coda	da capo, return to the beginning, play to the coda sign (𝄌), and skip to the coda
D.S. al Coda	dal segno, return to the sign (𝄋), play to the coda sign (𝄌), and skip to coda
Fine	end or close
Play 4 times	repeat as indicated

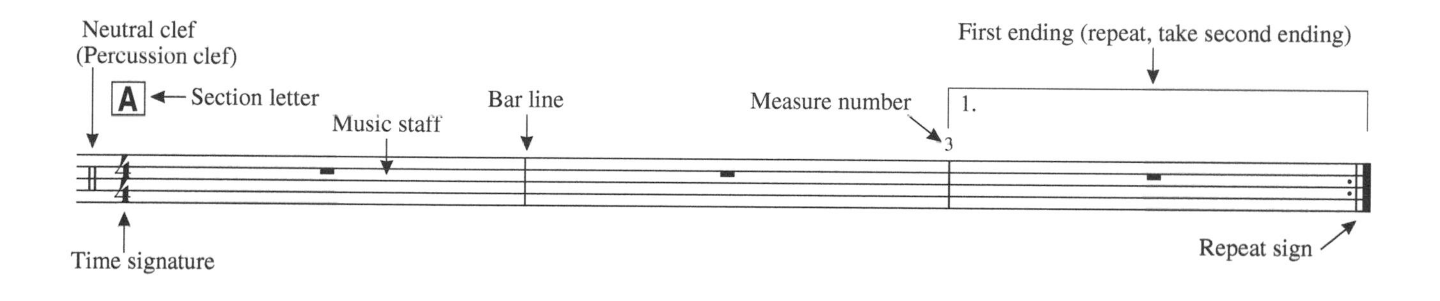

Notes

Notes